Roy Appleton

GROUP
LEADERSHIP

By Neely D. Gardner

National Training and Development Service Press
5028 Wisconsin Ave., N.W.
Washington, D.C. 20016
(202) 966-3761

Contents

Year by year there is an increasing interest in discovering how better to explore problems, learn, develop data, resolve conflicts, increase understanding, set goals, make decisions and obtain commitment to actions through the effective use of groups. This monograph is devised as a training guide to be used by persons who wish to improve their group leadership skills. It will explore questions concerning values, motivation, leadership and membership, dynamics of groups at work, communications, methodology and resources available.

1. Values and Motivation

Group leadership, as discussed here, refers to democratic rather than to charismatic or authoritarian behavior. Values involved are democratic values. The implied political theory is that the governing bodies, political or administrative, derive their just powers by consent of the governed. The democratic mode suggests that participation by those affected is a necessary prelude to intelligent consideration and willing consent. The democratic bias is for maximizing individual freedom. The types of leadership examined here reinforce the tendencies in organizations to provide for self-management on the part of the individual. The process further emerges as an attempt to help the individual discover the means for self-actualization.

Values

Even if these values were not stated the act of working together in groups to achieve organizational purpose tends to be a democratic, power distributing act. Whether the increasing utilization of groups is causing greater collaboration in our complex world or whether groups are being used because they are desperately needed in our over-specialized and highly developed society may be a moot question. Regardless of political leaning—right, middle or left—the tendency to meet, confer and decide in groups appears to be a modern necessity even though there are individuals in every political mold who resent and resist group effort.

The movement toward shared communication and decision

1

is world-wide: less in totalitarian than in more democratic societies; more in developed than in under-developed countries, but growing everywhere. We stress the value implications of group leadership here because one of the underlying values held for the group process is the value of openness. Those engaging in democratically-oriented group leadership activities should be aware of the values which may necessarily accompany the process.

Motivation

Persons contemplating developing greater group leadership skills might well try to determine "if it really works" and, if so, "why?" Researchers and theoreticians are still trying to answer these questions. By now the answer to "if it works" is not nearly as puzzling as "why it works." Nevertheless a body of knowledge is beginning to emerge which, if not giving "answers," at least permits rational speculation.

Human beings are goal-centered, the goals they set being conditioned by their needs. Individuals vary a great deal in their needs, but each perceived need is a motive to action until it is met, and meeting the perceived need is a goal. When people become aware of (when they perceive) an unmet need, they experience desire or discomfort which is only satisfied if the need is met. Thus:

Need + Goal = Motivation

Association with other human beings provides, on the one hand, a means of gaining assistance in meeting known or perceived needs and, on the other hand, an opportunity to discover new needs, set new goals and develop new motives. These discoveries are a result of sharing ideas that are beyond the range of one individual's experience and of exploring an expanded range of options which are available to the person for the achievement of goals. Both individual and group life is a process of conceptualizing, experiencing, experimenting and learning. Some needs cannot be met unless we collaborate with others. Some needs cannot be met because they conflict with the needs of others. By developing leadership and membership skills we try to become more effective in the process of collaboration and in utilizing means by which conflicts between ourselves and others may be resolved.

It will help perhaps if we now take some time to review the theories of the human need system and see how they provide for the motivation of the individual. There have been many investigations aimed at learning about human needs. The results of these investigations have been classified or categorized in a variety of ways, but in general they are mutually reinforcing. One such investigation that represents rather a central theme in need theory was conducted by Abraham Maslow.

Maslow's Hierarchy of Needs

Maslow, who conducted his unique research in a population of highly integrated and effective people, suggested that there is a hierarchy of human needs. It was his view that humans progress in their need-meeting behavior from a state in which they fill their basic and survival needs to one in which they strive to meet their more esthetic needs. Maslow categorized this hierarchy of needs in five levels:

Physiological or homeostatic needs. These are basic survival needs such as requirements for air, food, drink, procreation and shelter. If these survival needs are met human beings will perceive another, "higher" level of need, the need for safety.

Safety needs. The starving person is not likely to worry about hazards of the highway, danger of arrest or possible bodily harm. Hungry scavengers will gather their meals from unhealthy refuse with little thought of the health hazard involved. Desperately thirsty people are not particular about the purity of water. History is filled with illustrations of men and women who have lost or endangered their lives in seeking out their paramours with flagrant disregard for safety. One familiar romantic example was the apparently desperate need of Leander, who nightly swam the treacherous Hellespont to be with the beautiful Hero. If people's physiological needs are sufficiently satisfied safety becomes a major factor. Then human beings begin to worry about germs, floods, assault and traffic. This worry causes them to devote energy, thought and effort to making the world safe for themselves.

Maslow noted that man's satisfactions are but temporary, and if the individual develops a feeling of sufficient physiological well-being and is comforted by feeling safe another need begins to intrude, and a person begins to experience the terrible chill of loneliness.

Belonging needs. One of our most compelling needs is to associate with others of our kind. Homo sapiens are social creatures. Without commingling with other human beings they become lonely. Next to physical torture the most cruel and devastating punishment a person may undergo is solitary confinement, away from fellow humans. Under such circumstances people frequently lose their minds and often even perish. The mental well-being of Robinson Crusoe certainly improved when Friday moved in on the island. Often people will undergo humiliation, hard physical labor and even psychological rejection if they are but allowed to "hang around" and associate with others. Thus the group "scapegoat" will endure a humiliating lot just for the privilege of being able to be with the group. But when associational needs are met, once we have achieved a place within a group, however menial, we begin longing for esteem.

Esteem needs. While people need the esteem and approval of others the important factor resulting from this is self-esteem (Fromm, 1950).[1] Eric Fromm believes that to be able to love and esteem others we must be able to love and esteem ourselves. On the other hand we require the love of others to develop love for ourselves. Very early in life we begin to develop an "as if" personality (Sullivan, 1953).[2] We begin to see ourselves and to behave "as if" we were as the mothering person sees us. Our self-concept and self-perception is conditioned strongly by the messages we receive at a very early age from our immediate and important associates. The fortunate persons are those who from the start develop a high degree of self-esteem. While there is a continuing struggle for people to reaffirm their estimability theirs is a lesser struggle than that of those ridden with self-doubts.

4

Even with such self-esteem individuals need continuing evidence from associates of the esteem these associates hold for them. Each person devotes a great deal of time attempting to elicit the approval of associates. Perhaps most of us become so involved in meeting our esteem needs, while maintaining a balance in our physiological, safety and belonging needs, that we never rise beyond this point. Those persons who do may only do so sporadically, for the next level of need in our society is the self actualization need, and for many of us fulfilling this need is only a distant possibility. The number of self actualized people among us is tragically small.

Self actualization needs. Self actualization becomes the goal for those who have achieved a strong feeling of self-worth. They feel loved and esteemed and have that warm inner feeling of being of value and worth—in other words worthy of love and esteem. They therefore turn their attention to creative lines of activities which are satisfying to themselves. The self actualizing person knows, as Shakespeare notes, that "virtue is its own reward." The struggle is no longer for approval that is either taken or given by others; the effort rather is to create and accomplish in a manner that pleases oneself. If Fromm is correct the person who loves him or herself will indeed love others and will feel a great sense of responsibility for society. His or her contributions to him or herself will also enhance the well-being of others (Maslow, 1954).[3]

Theory X and Theory Y

Another theoretical position related to human motivation is the important and well-known exposition of Douglas McGregor on Theory X and Theory Y. McGregor points out that there are two views of the nature of humans which influence the way leaders behave and which impact the degree to which workers in an organization are motivated. These same assumptions are applicable to collaborative effort undertaken in a group (McGregor, 1960).[4] One view, Theory X, is that people are venal and irresponsible; the other, Theory Y, is that they have a desire to use their potential.

- Under Theory X we assume that:
  1) People are essentially lazy.

5

2) They avoid responsibility.
3) Unless coerced they will do nothing.
4) The leader bears the burden of the performance of his or her followers.

• Theory Y indicates that:
1) Work is as natural as rest and play.
2) People have a desire to use their potential.
3) If people understand and accept objectives they will exercise self-direction and self-control in achieving those objectives.

Under Theory Y there is no need to control and coerce. The motivation is already present and the role of leadership is to create an environment in which the potential human energy can be released. Much human potential is wasted because many forces that impinge on individuals in organizations and in groups are constraining rather than driving forces.

Kurt Lewin was concerned about these forces as they effect change, and in developing his field theory came up with the notion of force field analysis.[5]

Force Field Analysis

The force field analysis is a powerful, analytical tool that can be utilized in decision and change processes. It has a place in group theory because it helps us comprehend how participative groups develop an understanding of the situation and adopt a willingness to change. Lewin felt that change involves three steps: 1) unfreezing, 2) exploration and 3) refreezing.

The unfreezing process is the process by which people begin to realize that change is desirable. For example, in the event of a riot, an epidemic or other major dislocation it can be expected that people's attitudes will be challenged, examined and shaken. There will be a period of readjustment in their thinking, feeling and perception. Then attitudes will settle down temporarily at another level and behavior will be modified to the extent that a change has taken place. The factors that influence the change make up the force field.

If one assumes, as Lewin did, that behavior can be viewed as normally occupying a semistationary level (however temporary) then this state of "valence" is maintained by "positive" vectors, which are constantly moving a person or group toward change, and by "negative" vectors, which are working against change.

Let us take as an example a city manager who wishes to organize the employee resources in his city so that services can be provided more effectively and economically. To help him in his efforts he meets with his department heads so that they may help decide the type of changes that are required and determine the nature and magnitude of such changes. In this situation it is possible for the city manager and department heads to examine the force field which impinges upon the city organization. It is also possible for them to proceed without systematically cataloguing positive and minus vectors. Whether the manager and department heads take the conscious approach or whether they consider the situation subconsciously, driving and restraining forces are nevertheless real and have a bearing on the action to be taken.

To develop a feel for the city manager's situation it might help to speculate about some of the impinging factors in the environment. For example, there appears to be an incipient trend in modern organization away from the *mechanistic* (bureaucratically structured) organizations and toward *organic* (problem-oriented rather than function-oriented) organizations.

In an organic structure able employees can be assigned to solve problems and deliver services on a project basis without regard to organization charts or boundaries of functional departments. In such an arrangement a fire captain might be assigned to head a housing project charged to prevent deteriorating housing and prohibit dilapidated housing from existing in the community. On the fire captain's project team there might be engineers, social workers, policemen, health inspectors, financial advisors and clerks. As the problem changed the nature of the work would change and so would the composition of the team. If the project's objectives were achieved the project team could be disbanded and the employees allowed to work on other projects where their talents could be used to a maximum degree. The theory is that an organic structure can

7

focus more sharply on objectives and output and less on organizational maintenance and ministerial activity, which is inherent in the mechanistic mode.

The city manager in our example is attempting through group methods to work with the department heads in examining the *organic* type structure as a change option. Before such an idea can be implemented it will also have to be worked through in some manner by the city council. There are obviously many factors favoring such an option, but there are also factors which are working against such a change. Here is a partial detailing of how the force field might look:

Force field analysis of an action option on how to change the city's organizational structure to an organic type in order to stimulate a more effective and economical delivery of services to our citizens:

Restraining Forces	Driving Forces
1. It is customary to organize bureaucratically and hierarchically.	1. Money is short for the city services.
2. Employees wish to keep their own domains. (Police do not wish to combine with fire personnel.)	2. Taxes are going up.
	3. Services are often not visible when housed in functional organizations.
3. The public cannot get very excited about reorganization.	4. Employees are stimulated by new challenges.
4. Councilmen will make enemies and not gain friends by supporting reorganization.	5. Reorganization often revitalizes operations simply by providing a "new look."
5. No one knows how the new type of organization would work.	6. Resources can be allocated on the basis of needed expertise rather than by function.
6. Employees are reluctant to work in ambiguous situations.	7. Organic type organizations are more flexible than are bureaucratic types.
7. The organizations are disruptive.	

If the city manager and his staff are to change organizational structure in city government they will need to diminish the influence of the "negative" vectors (restraining forces) and reinforce "positive" vectors (driving forces). By so doing the semistationary balance of factors maintaining the present organization will be unfrozen. Depending upon the strength of the constraining and driving forces a new kind of organization structure will emerge. (Normally the police and fire departments carry too much political "muscle" to move them out of functional type organizations, and therefore as a constraining force this political muscle cannot be neutralized. The rest of the city departments might not, for example, be so politically entrenched.) Since it is unlikely that all constraining forces can be removed and all positive forces enhanced the new "valence" will probably provide less than total change, and the new city organizational structure will be frozen accordingly (i.e., all parts of the city organization will be structured on a project basis except for police and fire services, which remain structured functionally).

A knowledge of field theory enables a group to examine its own decision process systematically as well as giving group members a useful means of examining substantive issues. They are permitted to look for causal factors behind the problem (Napier and Gershenfield, 1973).[6] Utilizing a participative approach in which leadership is shared permits group members to set goals, define problems, gather data and decide on desirable courses of action. The process itself thus becomes an unfreezing, change producing process. A force field analysis encourages investigators to examine problems in a more systematic and understandable way.

Field theory is related to, but different from, general systems theory, which also has application to the group leadership process.

General Systems Theory

In its abstract form a "system" as conceived in general systems theory involves:

1) input—energy, manpower, materials, technology and information which are provided from the external environment,

2) process—the activities with which the organization con-

9

verts resources derived from the input into some kind of product,

3) output—the goods and services produced by processing the resources which have been provided by the environment and

4) feedback—information to and from the environment about the quality or quantity of the output. Through feedback the system is set to act upon and thus change the environment, and the environment acts upon and changes the system.

Any system may be thought of as "an organized or complex whole, an assemblage or combination of things or parts forming a complex whole." (Johnson and Kast, 1963).[7] Except perhaps for the universe every system is a subsystem of a larger system. Governments are systems, organizations are systems, and groups are systems. A simple model of a system would look like this:

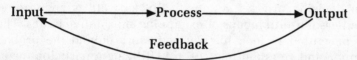

The actual interaction of a subsystem with its environment, however, is much more complicated. Magoroh Maruyama advances the notion that the unintended consequences deriving from a subsystem can be, and often are, more impactful than the intended consequences "deviation amplification." (Maruyama, 1963).[8] Almost any system provides examples of such deviations. For example, the great freeway and beltway systems have contributed to the growth of suburbia, the exodus from the central city and the scourge of smog. The space program has contributed "teflon" which has revolutionized the pots and pans industry, not to mention dishwashing processes in the home.

We have been discussing general systems theory in the abstract, but the theory has interesting implications for understanding the actual forces at work in groups.

Inputs to the system are made largely by people along with any technology (libraries, reports, audio-visual equipment, information materials, meeting rooms, etc.) Each participant brings a set of knowledge and skills to the group. Group members also bring values, biases and a variety of personal agendas. More importantly, perhaps, people bring feelings about themselves and others that have great influence upon how they behave themselves and interact with other members. Each person comes equipped with individual and unique defenses to cope with frustration or perceived attack. In addition, each person brings a number of roles that he or she occupies in other settings (i.e., mother, wife, golfer, club person, church member, etc.). Each role conditions the nature of a participant's input.

Processing these inputs involves complex activities (to be covered more thoroughly under the heading of "Dynamics of Groups at Work" which includes leadership and participation; communicating and listening; decision making, conflict, "goofing off," dealing with procedures, substantive issues and feelings; and establishing status and assuming roles within the group.

Group *outputs* are multiple. One product is the implemented decision. Another is the degree of commitment of group members to seeing that the decision is successfully carried out. Another important product is the understanding developed by each individual participant concerning group objectives implied in the decision and the reasons therefor. Finally each member develops a level of trust which will help or hinder the implementation of the decision.

Feedback will come to the environment from group members. Attitudes toward the "product" will be developed by client groups. The impact of a decision will be noted formally or informally. Individual group members will evaluate the outcomes differently, often being influenced by their "original" prediction on the efficacy of the group's decision.

There will be unexpected consequences, some of which may be recognized and some of which may not. Feedback will have a part in reeducating both the group members and those in the environment effected by the group.

In discussing inputs we mentioned "role" as a factor which influences human interaction. There is a growing body of knowledge in the area of role theory. Next is a summary of some of the concepts which are central to understanding role theory.

Role Theory

People are motivated to take on certain behaviors because of the stimulation of external and internal pressures attached to role. Role as used by sociologists and psychologists is somewhat similar to the definition given the term by dramatists. The concept of role is that of a "part" assumed by an individual through accident of birth, "casting" by society or by the individual's choice. It is probably misleading to say that people play roles in the sense the word is used here, rather people in the course of living "take" various roles depending upon the situation in which they find themselves.

Role theorists are principally concerned with investigating patterned forms of behaviors involving (1) physical characteristics, (2) expectations, (3) group or societal norms, (4) specialization, (5) position and (6) status.

There are several ways of classifying roles. One useful approach is to classify roles in terms of *ascribed* roles (roles assigned to individuals with no reference to personality attributes or competencies), such as black, woman or Italian; or in terms of *achieved* roles (roles available to people on the basis of individual competency, assignment or choice), such as the roles of leader, follower, taxi driver, supervisor, mayor or actor.

Another way of looking at roles is whether the roles are *basic, general* or *independent.*

Whatever means are used for classifying or examining roles it helps to keep in mind that role theory is helpful to the extent that it leads to learning and understanding behavioral processes growing out of human interaction. Role theory, then, has considerable utility in helping us understand the group process. It might help if we took a look at some of the roles which are taken in the process of group interaction.

A primary role in the group is the leadership role. In order for a group to function well it must have effective leadership. This leadership need not, however, reside in one person. There is considerable evidence to the effect that the leadership role is best performed when it is shared. Thus one person at a given time may have most to contribute as a leader in a particular group situation. When this confluence of events prevails that person will take the role of the leader; when the situation passes, leadership may move to someone else. In groups leadership is sometimes described in terms of *task leadership* and *social leadership*. Task leadership helps the group examine substantive issues while social leadership pertains to the group process and group maintenance roles. In addition to the very important leadership role in the group there are other member roles which include the following:

1) *blocker*—person acting in a role which prevents the group from making progress toward stated goals,

2) *clarifier*—person helping group members understand what is being said or what is happening in the group,

3) *defender*—person coming to the rescue of those who are under attack from others in the group,

4) *initiator*—person developing and contributing new ideas or in some other way stimulating the group to undertake new directions,

5) *gate-keeper*—person helping the group "keep on track" and move toward achievement of group objectives and

6) *punisher*—person seeing that those who are "out of line" get told about it.

There are many other achieved roles that emerge in groups. Taking note of these roles sometimes can be useful in developing insight concerning behavioral patterns. Caution should be exercised, however, to avoid the danger of stereotyping group members.

An interesting name that has been given to the roles participants bring with them from "back home" as they enter a group is "the hidden committee." Hidden committees are made up of all the people in the groups to which the person belongs in other times and places and where the participant has an es-

13

tablished and perceived role. Sometimes the hidden committee works on values. At other times it may be very conscious of the well-being of the constituent group. The hidden committee member may be aware that the quality of decisions of the group will have a definite effect on his status in the "back home" situation — in the union, church, work group, etc. Understanding the roles that various members take outside the group can sometimes help bring about understanding of their behavior within the group.

There are some roles which people bring to groups which immediately influence others' behavior toward them. For example, working roles such as city manager, department head, engineer, attorney, supervisor or secretary will carry with them certain role expectations and demands. A city manager working as a member of a group wich involves subordinates may be seen in terms of the role perceptions the subordinates carry of a city manager, though the manager may see himself as "one of the boys." Unless status situations are recognized and dealt with they are likely to hamper group functioning.

There are a number of dimensions of role which are important to understanding both organizations and groups. The following concepts may be helpful in developing an understanding of motivational factors involved in role:

1) *Role Expectations* — the concept one has of a given role and the behavior appropriate to that role. (One would not expect, for example, that a clergyman would frequent a topless/bottomless night club.)

2) *Role Sending* — the verbal and the non-verbal messages we send others concerning our role expectations. (Little girls wear dresses and play with dolls.)

3) *Received Role* — the message the role occupant receives from the role sender in regard to the sender's role expectations.

4) *Role Behavior* — perceived behavior of the role occupant after processing and acting upon messages from a variety of senders as to the senders' role expectations.

14

5) *Role Conflict*—dissonance between the several roles taken by one individual. (Supervisors frequently find that their roles as subordinate, boss and peer are in conflict with each other.) The position in the middle has been called *inter-sender* where one is receiving at least two different sets of messages. Another area of conflict is that of *intra-sender* where two different messages emanate from the same person. A third role conflict is termed *inter-role conflict* where the sent expectations of one role of an individual are in conflict with those expectations of another role being taken by the same individual.

6) *Role Reciprocity*—roles that require each other such as: patient—doctor, client—lawyer, student—teacher, and child—parent (Katz and Kahn, 1966).[9]

7) *Role Set*—the cluster of roles that attach to any one individual.

Understanding the function of role and the elements of *role conflict* will help group members understand and deal with each other on realistic terms. In those happy instances when individuals achieve *role-congruity* (when there is no *self-role conflict*) group forces can be brought to bear on other needs and problems of the group, and the *role-congruity* makes it possible for group members to motivate themselves.

Most of the theoretical concepts of motivations covered here seem to relate to learning—to the normative, reeducative process. To understand the "why" of such concepts suggests a look at learning theories.

Learning Theories

There are many ways to learn: by emulating, by exercising the senses, by memorizing, by experiencing or by combining experiencing with immediate evaluation or feedback. Learning can be the result of both conscious and unconscious effort. Action research, for example, is a *conscious* process for producing learning results. A child touching a hot utensil on the kitchen stove illustrates unconscious learning. In each instance, however, it is clear that **PEOPLE LEARN WHAT THEY DO.**

15

One's theory of learning depends, at least in part, on the type of learning one is talking about. Since this monograph is examining group leadership our search is for information pertaining to learning in groups.

Motivation for learning generally depends upon the rewards the learner receives for succeeding and the punishments incurred for failing. It is possible to condition behavior if meaningful rewards and punishments are carefully and consistently administered, provided other influences do not intrude in a more compelling way. Skinner makes the point that most of us have had our behaviors conditioned to a much greater degree than we realize. Further, most conditioning has occurred through punishment. Punishment, he says, is less effective than reward because it causes aversive or avoidance behavior which forces compliance but stifles willing effort on the part of the person being taught. In his *Beyond Freedom and Dignity* Skinner makes a plea for a new type of conditioning which, he says, will create citizens who are well-integrated and capable of coping with modern problems (Skinner, 1971).[10] Presumably the conditioning would be done by honorable men who were sufficiently wise to foresee what kinds of behaviors would be desirable in the future.

While granting that many of Skinner's notions of *operant conditioning* are valid we believe that there are both theoretical and value questions involved. First, it may not be possible to condition human behavior totally because of each individual's ability to conceptualize. Secondly, each individual's environment is extremely complex and difficult to contain. Finally, the very personalized, incrementally formed and unique "private world" of each individual moves in unseen ways safely (at least for the time being) out of reach of the operant conditioner. But it may be that the value question transcends the theoretical. So we are justified in asking by what right do we "condition" our fellow man without a mutually agreed upon process where at least an individual becomes as much a conditioner as a conditionee?

In normative-reeducative terms mutuality exists because learner and leader are each a part of the developing situation in which involved persons explore the terrain and join in the search for solutions. Leader and learner are interdependent.

16

Given such an approach learning in a group is enhanced under the following conditions:

1) A person's awareness of the needs of others will assist the learning of both self and the others involved in the transaction.

2) Awareness establishes credibility to self and others.

3) Credibility is part of the process of establishing trust.

4) When a condition of trust develops differences can be tolerated.

5) Examination of issues and problems is made easier in a group in which awareness, credibility and trust are present.

6) There is normally a discrepancy between the environment as it actually exists and the environment as it is perceived by individual group members. Examination of issues and problems in a climate of trust leads to diminishing existing discrepancies in perceptions.

7) Under conditions of such open exploration the goals are intrinsic, and attempts to achieve these goals are successful or unsuccessful rather than being either rewarding or punishing. This may be because:

   a. "to reach a goal constitutes success,"

   b. "to get within the region of a goal may be a success experience since some goals are less well-defined than others,"

   c. "to make notable progress toward a goal may provide a successful experience even though the goal is remote" and

   d. "to select a *socially approved* goal may in itself be a success experience." (Hilgard, 1956).[11]

8) "The individual's level of aspiration is very much influenced by the standards of the group to which he belongs." (Deutsch and Kraus, 1956).[12] The aspirations or goals initially expressed in groups generally indicate a level above previous performance of that individual group.

9) Given awareness, credibility and trust groups are likely to aspire to and achieve higher goals, and the abilities of most

of the members will be valued and utilized increasing the available resources and therefore providing a more comprehensive base for learning.

10) In such a learning situation concepts, actions and decisions are advanced and tested while immediate feedback is given and received. Processing or "reality testing" performance against feedback enhances the learning of the individual involved.

2) There are other learning theories. One major grouping of theories might be called *reinforcement theory*. Reinforcement has typically utilized either classical or instrumental conditioning. Pavlov's well known experiment represents classical conditioning. For a time meat powder was placed in an experimental dog's mouth and he automatically salivated. In attempting to condition the dog a bell was rung just as the meat powder was administered. After the simultaneous feeding and bell ringing occurred for some time the meat powder was discontinued but the dog continued to salivate with every ringing of the bell. Thus the animal had been conditioned to respond to a secondary stimulus (Deutsch and Kraus, 1956).[13]

3) In instrumental and conditioning learning (E. L. Thorndike) the response to be conditioned must occur first, then rewarded or punished. Both reinforcement theories are described in the following terms:

1) *Response strength* — where the response tendency is measured according to
   a. probability of its occurrence,

   b. rate of responding,

   c. latency,

   d. magnitude and

   e. resistance to extinction.

2) *Extinction* — the decrese of response strength to non-reinforcement.

3) *Discriminative stimulus* — one which governs the occasion on which response will be reinforced.

4) *Reinforcement* — the happening that occurs after the response which leads to the response is being repeated. The main dimensions of reinforcement which researchers often address are as follows:

a. quality,

b. amount,

c. extent of delay (between behavior and reinforcement) and

d. scheduling and programming of reinforcement activities: rewards, punishment, secondary reinforcement and intermittent vs. constant reinforcement.

5) *Drive* — the underlying conditions that cause behavior.

6) *Generalization* — the situation in which the response to the "conditioned" situation is applied to similar situations (Deutsch and Kraus, 1956).[14]

2. Leadership and Membership

As discussed here leadership is considered to be a function which can be performed, either by one individual or a number of individuals in a group or organization. The leadership process is a process of influencing behavior and stimulating (group, organizational or governmental) activity. As a person who is leading I can influence myself, which is a simple but inportant thought. Beyond myself I might be able to influence others if I hold some "office," have a degree of expertise that is needed if I have control of desired resources or even if I have the backing of a group of "important" people. In the process of influencing others those who are led, the followers, may find new things to do or different ways to do them, be stimulated to the point of thinking creative and exciting thoughts or in some other way feel "liberated." On the other hand if my power to influence those individuals encroaches on their life space, they have to weigh the benefits that accrue from their followers' roles against the disadvantages that develop as a result of their loss of freedom.

If you follow me because of the position I hold — that is, the position of boss, parent, trainer or some other designated role — then you are likely to feel that you are being compelled to act even though you may not dislike the act itself.

Leadership and Role

Leadership that stems from my "role" as an institutional agent can, and often does, stifle and de-energize the follower,

21

or at least does not stimulate that person's active commitment, and certainly does little for unleashing creative ability. Nor does it generally permit me the advantage of the other person's knowledge, experience and competence unless the participant-follower is also placed in a leadership role. In such a circumstance both of us might lead.

Before you reject such a notion as conducive to the creation of group-oriented bedlam let us address the other sources of influence: *expertise* and *referent power.*

Expertise

If we are working together on a project to develop new energy sources and I am an authority on nuclear energy, you are an expert on political process and a colleague who is an M.D. is a specialist in environmental medicine, we are likely to be influenced by each other in regard to each person's area of expertise. With some luck and good will, we might even develop the ability to communicate to and learn from each other. Under these conditions leadership might be shifted from person to person. It would certainly be possible to move ahead more expeditiously if each expert's influence were mobilized. It would not be possible to utilize the potential energy and creativity of these experts without sharing the leadership role.

Referent Influence

Referent influence generally comes from outside the formal organization. Political overtones are attached to such influence. I gain my power because others see fit to support either me or my cause. There are persons in each group or organization who, though they may or may not be leaders in their own right, are in fact leaders because they are able to assist or impede collective effort. Such persons might be highly respected by their colleagues or they may be in a strategic position in one of the organization's communications networks. While not possessing leadership roles these persons might be in a position to supply or withhold support to those who do. Persons whose

22

leadership influence is based on referent power must always take note of the views and changing perceptions of persons who provide such power.

Designated leaders depending upon referent power might find it possible to share their leadership roles if the group with which they are working and the referent group are synonomous. The task becomes more difficult when a referent group is comprised of different individuals than the work or task group. In the work or task group it is possible, but difficult — even unusual — for persons operating from a referent power base to make the work group aware of the views of the referent population. A leader utilizing referent power has unique commitments to linkages and personal awareness of boundaries that are difficult to share with others in the group. The difficulty seems to stem from the nature of trust, rewards and promises which have grown out of transactions with the referent group. If it were possible to generate commitment, mutuality and awareness it might be possible for the work group to give consideration to the referent group's views on an open and shared basis. Generally referent power is by nature political and even on occasion manipulative.

Now we would like to make our definition of leadership more explicit:

"Leadership is a set of functions through which the group coordinates efforts of individuals." (Thelen, 1954)[1]

Expanding the definition in a way to include larger units and organizations we would take the Katz and Kahn view that "leadership is every act of influence on matters of organizational relevance." (Katz and Kahn, 1966)[2]

Circumstances Requiring Leadership

With these definitions it is possible to examine circumstances in which the performance of the leadership function is required.

Changes in the environment. For example, when the supply of fossil fuel is short, when the world supply of food is insufficient or when the air becomes dangerous to health we have a change in the environment which requires an exercise of leadership. But environmental shifts need not be so global, for at a lesser level, the turnover of key employees, the drop in city sales tax revenue or the election of a new majority in a county commission are all changes that require the exercise of leadership in the affected organization.

Incompleteness in organizational design. It is not possible to organize in a way which meets all contingencies. Organization charts, specifications, standard practice manuals and all manner of rules and regulations cover only anticipated situations. At best these instruments become stylized, abstract models that set forth the "shalt nots" and are only hazy guides to situations which require innovative behavior. It is the organic, not the mechanistic situation which requires leadership. Since the available guidelines are mechanistic and abstract only through the perspectives of individuals armed with knowledge is it possible to provide a realism in regard to the problem and to mobilize resources available to solve the problem. Perhaps the more pervasive the problem, the more that leadership should be shared with those who are affected directly.

The internal dynamics of the organization. In every organization there are conflicts, alliances and deviations brought on by different individuals taking different roles and carrying out wide ranges of duties in changing circumstances. For example, problems arise due to the differing perspectives held by officials in operating departments and by the director of finance. Another cause of problems might be the supervisor's view of a work situation differing with that of an aggrieved employee.

The nature of human membership in organizations. Obviously the need for leadership is made necessary because of individual needs of the complex human beings who make up the organizations. Employees, however committed and dedicated, spend only a portion of their daily lives in the work group. In terms of their private worlds employees are constantly intermingling work time and private time. It would probably be amazing, even frightening, to be able to tune in on the private thoughts and feelings rampant in an apparently calm and outwardly business-like work setting. We might come face to face with fantasies of a man or woman falling in love, of heartaches due to strained home relationships, of worry caused by burdensome debts, of visions of an anticipated weekend or of a thousand other euphoric, angry, anxious or trivial thoughts. Each of these persons, depending upon the strengths and drama of events in these private worlds, invests or withdraws from the world of work. At any one time the amount of a person's life-space occupied by his work world represents only a portion of that person's available life-space. And while the life-space expands or contracts in day-to-day activity, in a more long-range perspective the individual is developing or deteriorating. He is learning, maturing, becoming apathetic, aging or changing in some other way. Humans are not cardboard nor even plastic. Feelings, flesh and blood, knowledge and energy make each human unique. Coordinating the efforts of these unique individuals demands leadership, and given the private and unknown dimension of many of the private worlds it seems reasonable that not only shared leadership but the opportunity for even greater self-leadership is important.

Collaboration

Uniqueness and individuality suggest the need for groups to collaborate. To each association from which I obtain something (a good) I may owe something (a good). If I give and do not receive my bank account may dwindle. In some manner I will pay a price in self-respect, health or development and renewal. In some manner there is an exchange of "give and get." Leadership and membership are inseparable. They are both "giving and getting" activities. Groups, organizational leaders and members, when performing to good purpose, act as if they are operating within the letter and spirit of an agreement (Thelen, 1954).[3] In the final analysis each individual will operate within the broad framework agreed upon by those with whom he or she is associating or reject the group. the organization, the formal and informal leaders. This acceptance or rejection may not be apparent from overt behavior, but even with an "aye sir" and a smiling face a rejection may be present. If rejection is present it will take its toll in human spirit, creativity and perhaps even in routine performance. The binding force of interpersonal transactions is the agreement or psychological contract. In democratic leadership the leader's function is to work toward creating a situation which permits individuals to stimulate themselves causing energy release and self-motivation. The question is "how can such leadership develop?"

Except in rare instances leadership in the early life of an organization or group may be a function of the formal or designated leader. It is clear that the designated leader has an essential role which in larger aspect calls for activity which attempts to obtain agreement on limits, assist the group or unit in achieving legitimacy, provide a safe situation for communication and learning and demonstrate behavior which is useful as a model. Such a role calls for:

1) Helping the group define, understand and become committed to its "area of freedom." In a task or training group the "area of freedom" coincides to some degree with the "charge" of the group. In an organization the "area of freedom" theoretically would be circumscribed by the mission statement, organizational norms, available resources, the degree of power in the work unit and the extent to which authority has been delegated—formally or tacitly.

2) Helping the group in "gate-keeping." This is acting as sort of a conscience to the group in terms of the agreements the members have made, the necessity of confronting and solving conflicts and the processes of learning and leveling in communication.

3) Behaving in a manner that models openness, listening and leveling and avoids catering to dependence tendencies that may be in the group.

4) Being trustworthy and working at trusting (Gibb, 1971).[4]

5) Providing opportunity for persons in the group or organization to maximize self-determination and self-assessment.

Shared Leadership

In shared leadership the group leader introduces processes and procedures which make possible and encourage participation. There is a wide range of methods available for use in participative groups. It is perhaps true that the more skill the designated leader develops (and by and by the other participants, also) the greater will be the creativity and productivity of the group. But technique will not save the person with an "evil" heart. Designated leaders, particularly administrators and trainers, must "prove" to their groups again and again that they believe in and wish to facilitate the legitimate participation of group and work unit members. Belief is not apt to emerge unless participants see their involvement as being helpful, meaningful and influential.

The group and the leader engage in a number of collaborative efforts including the effort to agree upon an acceptable agenda. The agenda should be one which members perceive as being in their area of competence. It also should cover a matter which is of interest to them. Through shared endeavor (leadership) the agenda is invested with meaning and the belief develops within the group that the energies being expended are worth-while. Finally the group must have confidence that the work it is doing will have an impact and is not simply an exercise. If the problem is interpersonal within the group members need to feel that they are competent to help, that it is worth-while to work on the problem and that as a result of group interaction some useful change will result. Likewise in attempting to solve an organizational problem group members must feel that they have the capability to help, that their assistance is meaningful and worth-while and that their efforts to solve the problem will have real impact and influence.

This all suggests that the success of a group action depends a great deal on the feeling of responsibility engendered in the group. In successful groups one could say that 1) internal and external expectations for group success must be felt by the group as a whole, 2) meeting internal and external expectations depends upon the definition placed on these expectations by the group members, 3) data required by the group are generated by the group members, and much of these data grow out of the experience of the group, 4) the group as a whole feels responsible *to* someone (person, client, community, etc.) as well as *for* something and 5) the responsibility felt by each member is for the need to cooperate and participate.

What Leadership Contributes

Ultimately leadership should assist in creating a situation which provides an opportunity for the release of energy of each group member and which stimulates innovative and creative outcomes. Group outcomes are enhanced when the freedom of the individual is increased. Collaboration grows out of mutual perceptions which are based on norms developed as the product of group growth. Actions of the designated group leader should assist or at least permit individual growth. Status differences built on formal position or social standing are reduced by the advent of a norm of mutual acceptance and respect. Acceptance and respect require caring as well as careful listening and the development of the ability to communicate authentically our own feelings and our own perceptions and of permitting others to glimpse and appreciate our private world.

In creating an environment for learning, communicating and caring leaders not only model behavior but also encourage the development of common experiences through group interaction. A period of group life is consciously devoted to becoming acquainted, first with others, then with oneself in relation to others. Getting acquainted does not seem to occur in any significant way through "ritual" introductions. Acquaintanceship occurs by participating as a group in activities that evoke "behavior" which can then be looked at consciously in "cause and effect" terms by those who are there—those who are doing the "behaving." Taking action, then giving and receiving feedback on the action increases awareness and provides closer acquaintance with oneself and with others.

Trust develops only marginally through the conceptual process. Trust development requires experimentation and testing as well. In fulfilling his trainer role, a leader, in addition to modeling trusting behavior, may encourage and contribute to a discussion of the concept of trust. There is little value in "talking about trust" unless individuals decide to experiment with trusting behavior. If a person trusts and is gratified by the results that person will then be able to trust more. If one is hurt by his trusting experiment one's trust development is likely to diminish.

28

Leaders (and managers too) are basically trainers. Training involves assisting group members in developing some personal, if tentative, theories about what they are trying to do. Given these theories participants need to acquire the skills which enable them to undertake the action. With skills plus theory a situation is generated in which members "behave" and experiment. By evaluating the results of their experiments group members are able to learn and grow. If the actions they undertake are within their personal capabilities range they will trust themselves more and be willing to risk more under similar circumstances that occur later. Group leaders provide procedural approaches (these may be training exercises or structured experiments) through which the learning occurs. As a trainer the leader encourages group members to assist each other in conceptualizing, developing skills and giving and receiving feedback.

The Dilemma

While the ideal situation is one in which shared leadership prevails society as well as individuals have some growing to do before this condition will exist. Some of us with starry-eyed expectations have attempted and failed to bring off fully participative organizations. We have made the mistake of assuming that by "delegating" with the honest intent of encouraging employees to order their own affairs, that true participation would take place. What we overlooked was the fact that in present day organizations people still participate, not by right, but by permission. "The Lord giveth and the Lord taketh away" is still the law of the organization. Bosses who have the right to delegate also have the right to withdraw delegation. Even in the best participative management efforts the permission to participate is given by the person or persons who have control over resources, personnel systems and organizational policy.

The authority habit is so ingrained in us by our parents, schools, social system and work organizations that "subordinates" simply cannot take on faith the notion that they are in charge of their own portion of organizational turf. This is reflected in the vocabulary of organizations with such words as boss/subordinate, higher-up/underling, chiefs/Indians, front office/trenches. This very language reinforces the authoritarian concept in each and every turn. With the ever-present reality that they are operating within the sufferance of the hierarchy which portions out resources, has the power to reorganize and can alter the promotional and salary structure, it is little wonder that employees view the voices and opinions of bosses and designated leaders as "more equal" than their own. Attempts to diffuse organizational power conflict with deeply ingrained dependency habits. Real opportunities to participate are often looked on as window dressing and even dangerous to those employees who stick their necks out and begin to exercise initiative. Thus the formal leader is constantly viewed with suspicion and is subject to having his role in the shared leadership process tested again and again. Theory Y leadership is probably accurately described as the most difficult management style one could undertake.

If we recognize that participation-by-permission differs from participation-by-right then we can better understand why the shared leadership function is complicated but by no means impossible. Let us say at this state we are moving *toward* participation and self-management. Knowing that formal leadership will be used as an unconscious excuse for dependency the effort may still be successfully made to diminish dependency and increase interdependency, to move toward shared leadership and away from unilateral leadership. By the effort to encourage shared leadership and self-management a great deal of freedom may be gained by the individual. Accordingly he will achieve more autonomy and have the opportunity to contribute helpfully, meaningfully and with influence to those work problems which affect him. There is a growing conviction on the part of many that we will never achieve our ideal of political democracy without also embracing an industrial democracy (Borgese, 1972).[5] Borgese says, "The theory and practice of self-management is likely to catch the imagination and mobilize the activities of hundreds of millions of people all over the world during the last quarter of our century." Society need not be the sole beneficiary of such a democratic development. There is much evidence to indicate that the energy released through this "partial" participation is highly beneficial

30

for the organization. Far more important to those concerned with freedom and the rights of man, the move toward self-management is enhancing the individual, which should be motivation enough even without the other attendant benefits.

There are many forces at work in groups, and the goals of shared leadership and enlightened self-management are enhanced by the knowledge of the group process.

3. Dynamics of Groups at Work

Group activity has been scrutinized through science-oriented eyes for at least the last 35 years. We now know a great deal about group forces and group process. It is clear that each group is unique, with behavior influenced by so many obvious and hidden variables that even the most practiced and sensitive observer does not see all. Even so, much that goes on in a group is predictable, not necessarily in the sense of when certain types of activity will occur nor which group members will be involved in specific activities at specific times, but in the sense that certain processes will occur during the span of a group's life. True, many phases of group life occur more strikingly in laboratory type groups than in work groups. But all groups which work together for a period of time tend to manifest many of the same behaviors as do laboratory groups, even though events and processes in work groups may be a bit more obscure. Some dimensions of the group process which help us in an understanding that forces that work in groups are *structural dimensions, stages of development* and *behavior modes.*

Structural Dimensions

Groups may be said to work simultaneously at three levels: *procedural, substantive* and *feeling.*

Procedural Activity. Groups operate according to certain procedures which may be either consciously determined or derived through happenstance. To clarify this notion let us consider a few significant and interesting group procedures:

- People tend to stake out their own physical territory when left to operate in an unplanned way. For example, they sit in the same location at each meeting. This may occur in staff meetings week after week. (If a leader calls the group's attention to this behavior and suggests that it would help the interaction if persons shifted positions each session that would be a procedural intervention by the leader.)

- Groups may arrange themselves in open circles or sit around long, narrow conference tables.

- Groups adopt certain patterns of communication. For example, everyone directs attention to the leader and the leader in turn talks to group members one at a time; or the group may "go round the circle," with each person talking in succession; or group members may discuss issues in a more conversational way.

- Some groups decide to start promptly at the appointed hour. Others are casual about starting times.

- Group members may give "speeches" at one another rather than communicate together.

- Listening is a norm in some groups while in others everyone talks at once and few listen to what others are saying.

- Leadership is sometimes authoritarian, sometimes facilitative and sometimes nonexistent.

- Members may let the group know where they stand on important issues or may remain silent as to their positions.

- Group members make jokes, engage in frivolous behavior, range toward the serious and business-like or operate with a range of such behaviors.

- Some groups may consider carefully the contributions of even the less active group members. Others may attend only to the more vocal or more influential.

- Some groups evaluate happenings in their sessions as to whether these forward or inhibit the group's efficiency. Most work groups do not.

- It is the norm of some groups to deal with conflict openly and for others to smooth over or repress conflict.

- Some groups vote, some arrive at decisions by consensus and some never decide.

- Some groups become so enamored of the group process that they spend most of their time looking at feelings. Some are strictly "product-oriented" and do not admit that feelings exist.

A complete list of procedural activities in groups could be almost encyclopedic. But procedures are a major determinant of the type of behavior that will be evinced by any group.

Substantive Activity. When a group addresses itself to the "stated agenda" it is engaging in substantive activity. A group brought together to learn about the functioning of groups might spend a great deal of time looking at itself. Most of the group's attention would be directed to what was going on in the group "here" at this time (the "here and now") rather than to problems and events occurring on the job back at the office (there and then). Solving work problems, making decisions, learning either subject matter or skills are all part of the substantive life of the group. Substance may therefore be broadly interpreted. It should be quite apparent to even the most casual observer of groups that the declared purpose of these groups is to function in substantive areas, but even in the most focused of groups there are side trips, humorous interjections and a plethora of other events that take groups away from the substantive issues before them. This behavior follows partly from the procedures which the group is following, partly from the fact that perceptions differ as to what the issues are or at least ought to be, and partly from the feelings of members who are considering the issues.

Feelings. In the last few years people in the United States have begun to admit that human beings have feelings and that feelings are not dishonorable. In fact there are good arguments to the effect that it may be self-damaging to try to hide feelings; conversely, it might be extremely useful to surface feelings, admit them and deal with them realistically. In any event we

35

all have feelings, and like it or not our feelings influence our behavior and how we relate to others.

Stages of Development

In a group of 12 persons carrying about 12 unique sets of life experiences operating according to group procedures which may or may not be comfortable and dealing with an agenda which is perceived differently by each of the 12 there are continually being generated bundles of feelings which each of the 12 must deal with in some way or another. It isn't enough that each person must deal with his own feelings, but every person in the group must relate to and contend with the behaviors generated in others. Even more these 12 sets of feelings are fluctuating moment by moment as the activity of the group proceeds. Each of our 12 possesses a unique private world which interprets and filters what he ingests from the world around him. So to be engaged in group or any other interpersonal activity and not be aware of the emotional content of the interaction is to operate in ignorance of the totality of forces at work.

The three structural dimensions are apparent during all stages of group development, (dependence, counter-dependence and interdependence) although the focus may differ from stage to stage.

Dependence. If we again assume for purposes of understanding that our 12 participants carry with them the burdens of their 12 private worlds and are faced with the inevitable responsibility of operating in tri-dimensional terms (procedures, substance and feelings) then it is understandable that these persons look around for some person to lead them. Most of our 12 will have to wait for the designated leader to be identified if this has not already been done. They will do this because they have been conditioned to expect that some person will call them to order, pass out the agenda and tell them how to proceed. It does not matter too much if the leader is drawn by lot from among their own number or preselected by some authority. He or she will be looked to for guidance simply because the person has been designated the leader. With such expectations imagine the consternation that occurred in some of the early group dynamics sessions when the leader, if that person said anything at all, was likely to start the session by the succinct statement, "We are going to be meeting together for the next two weeks. We are going to try to learn from each other and from what goes on in this group. How the group uses its time is up to the group. Now, perhaps, you might like to get started."

In the days before knowledge about groups became fairly widely disseminated this leadership behavior came as an intense surprise. The reaction of the members was one of stunned disbelief. Usually the leader's short remarks were followed by a painful silence that seemed to go on and on and on. The group members would shift in their chairs, laugh nervously or stare into space in order to avoid eye contact with other members. Finally, to the intense relief of the group, some person who could no longer stand the build up of tension would typically begin asking the leader questions or divert the group with a bad joke that the group would find hilarious. Whatever the silence-breaking activity might be, it would not take long for some of the group to begin bombarding the leader with questions which would be around the issues of "why are we here?" "how do you expect us to proceed?" or "we need to hear a little more on what we are expected to talk about." The leader, trying to keep out of the dominant role, would not answer these questions directly but smile and say something like, "You're really puzzled as to our purposes for being here and would like to know what to do next."

Twelve private worlds would be in turmoil. Some participants would get angry, some would withdraw, others would try to take the "bull by the horns" and get the conversation started.

One group of worlds would probably be thinking, "The leader must be able or he or she would not be here. The leader will let this thing go on for a while and then will straighten it out."

Another set of worlds would be angry, "Here sits this toad trying to look like Buddha when he is supposed to be here training me. We've got to make him organize this group."

What seems to be happening in such a case is that group members are showing their dependence on authority. They wish to be told how to behave, and in their view it is the leader's job to do the telling. During the first stages of group life, in this culture at this time in history, we can predict that group members will initially react in a dependent way toward the leader. In cases where the leader is far more active than in the extreme illustration given here group members will look to the leader, will not take responsibility for group action, will ask questions of the leader and will attempt to make most of their comments to the leader and not to each other. Many individuals will be hesitant to speak up because of the fear of standing out in relation to other group members. In work groups in organizational settings this dependence on the designated leader, the boss, is even stronger.

It can be predicted with some accuracy that group growth will be retarded or even arrested if leaders nourish or compel the continuance of the dependency feeling. If the leader is aware of the feeling the leader can discourage it by referring questions and problems back to the group. When group members finally become aware that the leader is not going to lead, both their anxiety and their anger mount. The members then move to the second and somewhat more uncomfortable stage of group development. In psychological terms this second stage is called counter-dependence.

Counter-dependence. Hostile acts may occur against the leader and other group members. Satisfied that the designated leader is going to "shirk" his or her duty there will be a move to exclude the leader. Groups will go on interacting as if the leader does not exist. If he or she attempts a comment it will be ignored. If the leader does make a comment that is picked up by a group member that comment is likely to be attributed to someone else. On some occasions groups have actually asked the designated leader to leave, declaring that participants would actually operate much better without the leader.

Not that the group is doing all that well with its new independence. There will still be leadership problems. Not all groups go so far as to elect a leader, but there will be an attempt among group members to assume the leadership. It is al-

38

most as if, "Now that 'big daddy' is out of the way I'd better help this group out by taking over." Sometimes we even see a small drama enacted which goes something like this:

Alex: This group has to have a leader. Charles you look like an able person, why don't you take charge?

Charles: Why pick on me? I'm not the type. Someone else who knows more about these things should do it.

Alex: Well, then, how about you, Mary? You're pretty and you could get along with all of us.

Mary: That's a typical male chauvinist remark. Anyway, Alex, you started this, Why don't you do it?

Alex: We-e-e-ll . . .

Marvin: Yes Alex, you're the leader type.

Others: Yeah Alex.

Alex: Well O.K. I'll try it for a while.

A fair amount of veiled hostility has taken place in the exchange. Charles feels picked on, Mary doesn't like Alex's attitude and reacts, Marvin subtly attacks Alex with a remark about the "leader type." But Alex, who wanted to be leader all along, accepts the job with assurance. How stupid can one be? It isn't but a few minutes until Alex's input is being rejected, sometimes openly, sometimes angrily, sometimes just by being ignored.

Soon someone else may try to take over, not by the pseudo consent route used by Alex, but simply by introducing a topic and trying to pursue it. But this and like attempts to gain leadership will also fail. There will be more attacks and counter-attacks. Hostility may be vented in fairly genteel ways, but it will be there.

From time to time the designated leader will again be the target of the hostility. Group members will even occasionally talk about the leader as if he or she were not present. At some point the frustration of the group will become so intent that part of the members will attack the leader directly. The group will see that it is possible to express feelings against authority openly with being "struck by a bolt of lightning." Some group members will rise to the leader's defense.

Counter-dependency is reaction against authority. It resembles the love-hate relationship of an adolescent child to its parents. There is a longing for independence and an anger against the restrictiveness of authority. Accompanying this is a desire for more direction when this is not given. Under authoritarian leadership counter-dependency frequently develops in more covert ways such as slow-downs in factories, shoddy work on production lines, inattention to customers in retail stores or such activity as leaking "confidential" news to the press. Many such organizational guerrilla tactics grow out of counter-dependent feelings.

In an atmosphere in which group members learn that they may express themselves openly about authority there is a possibility of developing beyond the aversive type behavior that stems from authoritarian management. Participants may view the leader in a different light, learning to accept the leader's competencies as well as shortcomings. In other words they begin to see the leader for what he or she is—a human being. Further, by becoming aware of the costs of aversive and hostile behavior members begin to seek out allies and find the means to resolve differences. When this occurs in groups the person who has performed the leadership role of mirroring (holding up the group's own behavior so that it may examine itself) may find acceptance. In training groups the designated leader frequently models such behavior. The leader can recognize the group's progression toward a new level when members find it safe to listen to him or her as a person and to accept some inputs, to reject others but to treat all with consideration. By whatever happenstance, when participants have vented many of their counter-dependent feelings they are then able to come together as a group.

Interdependence. The stage of interdependence is reached when members begin thinking of the total group as an extension of themselves and of themselves as vital components of the total group. There is an increased degree of mutual respect among members. There is a willingness to help and to be helped. Cooperation tends to replace competition and acceptance to supersede rejection. More conflict is permitted in the group because the nature of conflict is understood and tolerated. As Gordon Hearne has said, the group has succeeded in its development to a very great degree when it permits its members to "go all different directions together."

Recalling that procedures, substance and feelings accompany each state of development one would expect the nature of these structural dimensions to change as the group moves from dependence to interdependence. In addition there are a variety of behavior modes that seem to be fairly typical of each developmental stage. These have been described by Bion, who characterized most behaviors evidenced in groups as being flight, fight, pairing and work (Bion, 1961).[1]

In trying to understand the forces that work in groups we now have three different perspectives:

1) _structural dimensions_ (procedures, substance and feelings),

2) _stages of development_ (dependence, counter-dependence and interdependence) and

3) _behavior modes_ (flight, fight, pairing and work).

Behavior Modes

Flight. Flight behavior is escape behavior. It evolves because of anxiety produced when the leader does not meet the expectancy needs of group members. Individual members do not have a sense of group direction. They do not know how to behave toward the leader nor do they know how to react to each other. No sense of boundary exists. Conjecture is concerned with:

1) How far the individual can go?

2) How long will the individual be on his or her own?

3) What are the risks and penalties for being "wrong?"

4) What will others in the group think?

A group's first reaction to ambiguity is to escape. Escape takes such forms as discussion of matters outside of the group,

41

"back home in the there and then." Members present case histories of events in their own lives and ask the group for solutions to the problem. This is safe enough since the group does not have a data base to solve the problem. Therefore advice and suggestions can be and are rejected. When group members do propose solutions it turns out that these approaches have been attempted previously and did not work. In addition to working futilely around case histories participants will also *talk about* setting goals for the group itself but will never get down to the business of seriously considering the substantive issues involved in goal setting. The distinction is between "talking about" and "doing."

Flight behavior is typified by self-orientation as contrasted with group-orientation. Rarely are there overt attempts to examine feelings, nor are effective efforts made to deal with substantive issues which fall within the group's "here and now" area of responsibility. At this point the group loves to spend time looking at procedural options, but somehow never gets around to their adoption. Election of the chairman, who should be leader, the nature of rules for discussion and the agenda are all matters which get talked about at length but do not get resolved.

There will also be side trips into irrelevancies including joke telling (as differentiated from joking behavior) and "war stories" (let me tell you what happened to me, you wouldn't believe it; or you should know how I heroically handled the situation and overcame it).

If the leader or the organization has not assigned or will not assign status to individuals in the group, the matter of status will be the genesis of even further anxiety. In a training group participants will make the effort to find out as much about the other person as they politely can. They will engage in getting-acquainted rituals: "I work for the Sun Oil Refinery—sales. What's your business?" "My wife and I have been married nine years. We have twin boys and a girl. The girl is the oldest and sort of a second mother to the twins. Do you have a family?"

In a work group, ritual inquiry will take place around such topics as neighborhood events, how someone is doing in the department and how the wife and kids are getting along. Almost all of the flight behavior is a demonstration to the leader or boss that nothing significant is likely to happen unless the boss caters to member dependency by stepping in and telling them what to do and how to do it. Otherwise it will take time for the group to find itself and this will only happen through a process of self-discovery.

Work-oriented groups and task forces match laboratory training groups in exhibiting flight behavior when they are told that the responsibility for development and action is vested in them. The words used may be different but the music is similar whether the work group is asked to determine what to do about developing the program for next year's budget request or when a T-group is charged with managing its own learning. In both cases the boss or leader will be badgered to answer questions about the organization's expectations. Flight in either the work or training group is a manifestation of dependent behavior (Bennis and Shepard, 1952).[2]

Group members will find it hard to believe that the leader does not have a plan. They will suspect that in some mysterious way the leader is guiding the whole situation so that in the end the leader's will is done. In the flight stage this opinion is usually voiced very openly. But the implication of flight-oriented action is that "we are wise to your little game" and will not be trapped.

While the flight mode is typical in the dependent stage of group development, some overly dependent individuals are flight prone. In any situation where tension creates anxiety this person is likely to (1) psychologically deny that tension exists, (2) change the subject to divert attention away from the source of anxiety or (3) rationalize or explain the situation in a manner that concludes that there is really no conflict.

There are also individuals who typically fight as a means of coping with anxiety. Frequently they appear to be bored when the group is moving along in harmony; but should an argument start, they lean forward in their chairs and charge excitedly into the fray.

Both those who fight and those who fly tend to manifest their

43

typical behaviors in each stage of group development but with their behavior being modified by the group situation. It helps to look on flight-fight behavior as "more or less" rather than as totally one way or another.

A group operating the flight/dependency/procedure pattern finds the tension to be so great that members frequently become hostile or apathetic. Fight begins to take over. The designated leader is overtly challenged. Participants blame the leader for the terrible state of the group. Deliberate acts of noncooperation occur. This moves the group into a fighting mode.

Fight. The group challenges the leader to clear up the mess. They say that the leader's ineptness will wreck the group or the organization's efforts. Secretly they suspect that the leader could bail them out. That makes them still more angry.

Lack of cooperation in the flight stage has caused still other reactions. People have paired (gotten together with one or more persons to seek comfort, agreement and support) and subgroups of participants rally to the support of "causes." Frequently members polarize around the issues of 1) let's develop a structure and plan around which to get things rolling (i.e., let's reestablish authority and hierarchy) or 2) let's "let it all hang out" and get involved in self-analysis or in everyone doing his or her own thing. A third or uncommitted group, usually made up of persons who have fewer authority conflicts tries unsuccessfully to mediate the conflict between the structuralist and the existentialist.

Pairing. One recognizes that pairing is occurring when alliances develop between people and polarization occurs in the group. Pairing also is visible when groups, faced with conflict and tensions, "fall apart" with little sub-subgroups beginning to caucus and talk to each other (Bennis and Shepard, 1956).[3] When the designated leader attempts to intervene or contribute the intervention is rejected, although members will still be saying that the leader should exert responsibility. If the leader calls attention to flight, fight or pairing, the group will deny the validity of the leader's observation.

As in the case of fight and flight some individuals exhibit

44

pairing-prone behavior throughout the group life. Repeatedly during meetings they engage in side conversations with fellow participants. In some ways those who pair consistently seem to have a need for recognition and support that they apparently do not always find in the group. It is as if they were with the group but not in it.

Fight and pairing are typical of a group in the counter-dependent stage. Participants will remain in the counter-dependent/fight/pairing stage, exhibiting but not examining strong feelings generated through group and interpersonal conflict. Fight/pairing will continue until the leader is symbolically removed from the group. Without the leader the group is ready, at last, to recognize the need for cooperative effort. Mediators who were previously ignored may now go to work within the group. After helping participants demonstrate their ability to resolve issues and to relate as a group of the whole, despite conflict and resultant disillusionment, members are then ready to operate cooperatively. Now that the group has wrested power and control for itself it can safely invite the leader or boss to contribute, but, of course, on the group's terms.

Work. When a group is working it is addressing itself to the achievement of goals, and these goals represent an accommodation of both group and individual aspirations. The group pursues these goals in keeping with acceptable and expected behaviors that have been developed through shared experience and unspoken agreement during the sessions. Work permits an examination as well as an exhibition of feelings. Work addresses substantive issues. Because the work mode fosters the achievement of both individual and group goals, the group has reached the state of interdependence.

To a participant in the midst of a developing group stages of development may not be as neatly discernible as this description might imply. Each meeting of the group might recycle the process in miniature. Just when the group gets going well it occasionally will have regressive periods when flight, fight or pairing are reestablished as modes of behavior. These periods are not usually leader-focused, but meet some immediate need as a group. For example, when a group has worked to physical or emotional exhaustion it is likely to engage in obvious escape through gossip, war stories or hilarious behavior.

By understanding concurrent interactions, stages of development and behavior modes, group leaders are provided with several approaches to understanding what goes on when people get together in groups — the forces at work in groups. In laboratory settings these forces emerge with characteristic clarity. Groups with a product or issue orientation also manifest these same processes. Expression of such processes is apt to be less sharply drawn in product and issue groups than is manifest in a theoretical description, just as a newspaper caricature of a well-known public figure differs from the flesh and blood person with that individual's more complicated, variable and dynamic self.

We may further our knowledge of group forces by trying to synthesize the three approaches we have used to look at groups. In the *dependent* state of development group members are likely to be more preoccupied in expressing themselves on procedures rather than on substance and feelings. They will take care, however, not to commit themselves to any given procedures. Substantive issues will most probably be discussed, but nothing will actually be done which leads to resolution. Feelings will run high as a result of ambiguity, but they will be carefully guarded. The behavior mode in the dependent stage will be largely flight.

When entering the *counter-dependent* stage groups give preference to fight and pairing. Participants will fight against ambiguity and are likely to polarize around procedural issues. Group members will try to initiate work on substantive issues, but no continuing agreement will be reached. Strong feelings will surface, but they will not be addressed directly. An independent group burdened by fewer authority problems than contending groups will fail in all atempts to mediate between viewpoints. Conflict will rage, but it will not be discussed, and perhaps its very existence will be denied.

Finally the group recognizes that there will be no intervention by formal leadership and begins to develop the notion that it has the capacity to regulate itself. It is as if the right to democratic leadership cannot be bestowed, but must be earned. When the group arrives at this point it is ready to *work*. Work equates with the independent stage of development. Work-oriented effort recognizes procedures and either abides by or alters them. Substantive issues are dealt with. Feelings are recognized as an important ingredient of group life and are expressed openly. If necessary feelings are examined and worked through. Conflict is utilized, not avoided. An effective group works procedural, substantive and feeling issues in a balance that maximizes both individual and group enhancement. Finally a group at work takes time to look at the group process. This enables the members to correct themselves and to improve work output.

Special Events

Certain events in group life tend to occur from group to group. Many of these events are neither sequential nor inevitable, but they occur often enough so that the leadership function is enhanced if the leader recognizes and reacts appropriately to them. (For want of a better name we are calling these *special events*.)

Without the claim that any one event is likely to be more important than any other, the following list includes some but by no means all of the more common events which occur in group interaction.

Conflict. Conflict occurs in a situation where opposite needs are in action. For example, I may need to choose between a desire to possess something and a desire to avoid a fight. Say that you and I, being hungry, both desire the last helping of food on the serving plate. I might very much wish to help myself, but I would also be concerned lest I hurt your feelings. Since I have high regard for you both the desire to help myself and the desire to please you create a conflict situation. The conflict occurs both between and within us. In another instance, I may have to choose between two "good" pieces of merchandise because I do not have the money to buy both of them. So another source of conflict would be the necessity to choose between two undersirable actions (the lesser of two evils). Brehm and Cohen suggest that the greater the number of alternatives from which one must choose, the greater the

47

dissonance following the choice (Festinger and Aronson, 1960).[4]

A group, "thrown" on its own resources and faced with working out its own destiny provides many opportunities for conflict. Conflict is manifest by outright argument or contention in which emotions can be displayed openly, or conflict can occur at a more subtle level with emotions being kept under cover. (I do not know why this suggests a cobra and its intended victim sitting smiling at each other.) Overt conflict normally does not occur until groups are moving toward the counter-dependent stage. Early in group life conflict is evidenced by such devices as ignoring the other person's point of view, asking probing and hostile questions, changing the subject or psychologically withdrawing from the group. Unresolved conflict may impede group development and prevent the emergence of caring relationships. Often differences are ignored. Sometimes other group members try to persuade contestants that their differences are semantic rather than real, as if semantic differences offer no opportunity for spectacular disagreements!

Conflict recognized and addressed can lead to greater development and understanding. Exploration of opposite feelings provides rich data which in all likelihood would not surface unless the conflict were openly joined. Recognition of the many opposite needs in action provides the group with an opportunity to increase its action options. When people air their differences with openness they do a great deal to help others to understand and to deal more realistically with the differences.

Hidden agenda. A great many persons come to meetings with expectations or agendas. These agendas are not "placed on the floor," but whenever the group is trying to move in any substantive direction these private or hidden agendas intrude on the action. If a hidden agenda appears to be enhanced by the decisions the group is making its owner will be supportive of that decision. If not its owner will likely oppose the proposal being considered. Frequently the arguments made by this individual against the proposal before the group are not explained in terms of the hidden agenda. In fact the hidden agenda frequently is not mentioned. If, however, a group member reveals a hidden agenda and this agenda is considered with respect it is possible to either meet that individual's expectations by incorporating them into group action or satisfy the person that those ideas have been thoroughly considered and that the group disagrees.

Referent groups. The National Training Laboratories made a do-it-yourself film in the late 1950's called *Our Invisible Committees*. In a discussion of roles of the various members it was pointed out that each person in the group belonged to several outside reference groups. Individuals take certain roles in each of the reference groups to which they belong. They carry as part of their psychological make-up memberships in a variety of groups, and their behavior is apt to be influenced because of these memberships. Therefore if I am a black in a black and white group I find myself taking a generic black role. As a woman in a man's group I am almost inevitably expected to take a woman's role. Being a black or a woman causes us to "represent" these referent groups even though we may declare that we are speaking as one unique black or as a specific woman. If the black should be a member of the Black Panthers or the woman a member of the National Organization for Women, the representation becomes more specific. Being a member of a referent group has two interesting consequences. First, my behavior is likely to reflect referent group norms (which may be in conflict with the norms of the present group), and secondly, I may feel obligated to represent my referent group, thus complicating the problem-solving capacity in the here and now.

The invisible committee becomes a greater issue in a work group which is striving to cope with organizational problems. A division chief or section head may be more concerned with pursuing a solution which would be to the advantage of his or her unit rather than devoting attention to solving problems of the total organization. Cabinet members and department heads rarely free themselves sufficiently from their referent group roles to enable them to take a global or "statesmanlike" view of the total organization's problems.

Silence. Groups frequently fall silent. Unless the silence is thoughtful and contemplative, as sometimes happens in groups which have reached advanced stages of development, periods of silence appear to provoke a rather high degree of anxiety. In the dependent stage of group life silence seems to be a form of avoidance. The dependent person silently might suggest, "If one doesn't speak one is not responsible for initiating action. In any case this group is not my responsibility. It is the responsibility of the leader. If he wants us to talk let him tell us what to talk about."

An early test of the leader often occurs at the very start of the session at the point where the leader turns the discussion over to the group. It is not unusual for a silence to occur at this time. If the leader does not fill the silence gap the anxiety level of group members will compel them to start talking. Such silent periods rarely exceed 30 seconds, but while they occur they sometimes seem much longer.

In counter-dependent moods groups may invoke silence as a deliberate means of punishing the leader for not providing a way out of the group's dilemma. Group members even enter into conspiracies of silence, getting together prior to the session and agreeing not to talk. During conspiratorial as well as other group silences body motion intensifies, breathing of some members becomes more pronounced, sometimes there is giggling or there is an effort by members to hide grins. Some members will cough and clear their throats. Accompanying the silence is a stubbornness that mounts as the silence grows. Some of this relates to an attempt to make the leader talk, if possible, before any of the group members talk. At the very least it is an effort to make the leader uncomfortable. Stubbornness also derives from the mood of contest, with no one wishing to be first to give in.

Generally the anxiety mounts to a level that exceeds the tolerance of some group member. In one conspiratorial silence recorded in a group a young woman broke the silence by beginning to sob. Every participant appeared to be intensely relieved, almost grateful that the tension was broken. "It was unbearable," the young woman said, "We all sat and sat and the silence became heavier and heavier. Every person here was silent but the leader was more silent than anyone else."

Feelings of relief are the usual response to the broken silence, and frequently the person breaking the silence will do so in a way to make that action seem inadvertent, such as coughing and excusing oneself, getting up for a drink of water and offering a drink to others, asking for a light for a cigarette or almost falling over in a chair that has been tilted back on two legs. It is not unusual for a group to make rather dramatic development after a silence. Nearly always a long silence provides a vehicle for examining the feelings which were generated.

As noted, not all silence is of a fight of flight nature. On occasion after group trust and solidarity have been developed members will fall into a contemplative mood. Such silences are comfortable and thoughtful. There are few non-verbal signs of group tension. Members feel free either to break the silence or let it prevail.

Fight and make up. Frequently when one member verbally castigates another during the meeting these persons will get together as soon as the meeting breaks up, usually in an effort to explain and ameliorate differences. In these making-up sessions the aggressor more often than not initiates the meeting. Sometimes the aggressor's motivation is defensive due to the realization that when one attacks there is likely to be a counterattack. By "explaining away" the initial hostility the more aggressive member tries to diffuse any latent anger that may reside in the one attacked.

Getting even. It is almost predictable that a person receiving criticism or a verbal barb from a fellow group member will, before many moments pass, "get even." Sometimes the getting even is direct. Often, however, it is a subtle action and may include such things as joining forces with other members in a demeaning, critical or disquieting rejoinder. On occasions the revenge takes the form of humor with the original aggressor being the butt of the joke.

Cyclical behavior. Groups, particularly those which meet in concentrated session for a period of several days, move in and out of tension-producing and tension-releasing moods. When a session has involved significant conflict or the examination of feelings, which has resulted in a high level of emotionality, the following session tends to deal with safer or more superficial issues. Sometimes these sessions even become frivolous and

51

irresponsible as if there is a need for rest and recreation from the fatigue that is often induced in a highly emotional session.

Protectionism. Some individuals react to others as if they were personally responsible for that specific person's actions. This type of relationship may occur in any group, but is more often seen when two colleagues are working in the same group or when there is a boss/subordinate difference. These one-to-one patterns may be manifest in the following ways:

1) The protected person will make a statement. The protecting person will interpret, embellish and reenforce the statement, assuring the group that "the protector's" statement is what the protected person really meant.

2) The protector will say about the person being protected, "Mary has done a lot of work in that area. Why don't you tell the group about it, Mary?"

3) The protector will put words in the protected person's mouth, "Is what you are saying that so and so, etc?"

Protectors are often the very next person to talk whenever the protected person says anything. Frequently the protector's words are in rebuttal but in polite and low key form. It is almost as if the protector were saying, "You are off the track and I have to straighten you out, but I shall still see that you look good before the group."

If I am involved in protectionism I may be, or at least feel, challenged by the protected person who, though close is of lesser status. If that person looks bad it reflects on me. On the other hand should the person perform too well it may jeopardize my position.

One-to-one protectionist relationships may interfere with the natural flow of the group since at least one and maybe both group members are somewhat immobilized by the contest.

Tyranny. It is possible for a few strong members to tyrannize a group. Tyranny can stem from the best of intentions. Those capable of tyrannizing a group usually appear to others to have established a power base within the group. Often the tyranny segment attempts to establish or strongly influence group norms. Frequently the tyranny sub-group has considerable insight in terms of desired group development activities but is coercive in its attempts to force the group to be developed whether it wishes to or not. Being correct does not lessen the tyranny. The process may best be understood with an example.

Let us say that persons forming the tyranny cluster are very much against another member's suggestion that the group as a whole be divided into sub-groups to address an issue. Let us assume that in this instance two-thirds of those present favor experimenting with the sub-groups, but each person is unaware of this feeling in the other group members. The remaining third, except for the tyranny group, probably couldn't care less. Big group, sub-group, it's all the same. By being vocal and definite in their opposition and by continuing their arguments even to the point of stalling the group around this procedural issue for several hours, they help leave the impression that their view is the view of the majority. The entire group then does not divide into sub-groups. The tyranny is successful because of a condition we might call pluralistic ignorance. That is, most members favor sub-groups but doubt that others do. Therefore they give up the struggle without testing the group opinion.

Sometimes one person who is willing to state his or her preference will cause an entire group to participate in activities that are of low priority to the group and not particularly useful for the development of the group as a whole.

Location. In adjusting to a group environment members will tend to seat themselves in the same location at each session. Location and physical setting have much to do with the nature of interaction. Persons seated opposite each other are more likely to communicate than those seated side by side. The former are also more likely to argue and oppose each other. Although the greater volume of communication from any participant is likely to occur across a circle or table pairing is more frequent with persons who are seated side by side. It is symbolic that our allies are typically on our side. It is not surprising that dramatic negotiations take place with deliberating nations sitting across the table from each other, nor is it surprising that labor sits on one side of the table and management on the other during bargaining sessions.

Arrangements which permit receiving non-verbal as well as verbal messages increase the quality of communication. Conference tables, while convenient for writing, seem to be a protective device for participants and also a psychological barrier to communication. Most tables limit eye contact to about half of the group. In cases where there is a head of the table or a place for the leader in the seating arrangement attention of the group tends to focus there rather than on the membership as a whole. It is also interesting to note that in cases where there is a blackboard or conference pad present the person who holds the marker or the chalk frequently becomes the group leader. The location of the charts and the blackboard becomes the "head of the table."

Interaction seems to be of better quality and distributed more equitably throughout the group when chairs are placed in a circle and when members change positions frequently causing them to interact across the room with a wider variety of people.

Rituals, symbolism and norms. Specific cultures develop in groups which work together for any appreciable length of time. These cultures include rituals, symbols and norms. In the broader U.S. society much personal identity attaches to occupation. Congenial with this sense of identity rituals reflect performance in establishing relationships which involve the exchange of occupational data. Even in groups in which participants are deliberately asked not to give information concerning their jobs and positions people apparently cannot resist the urge to describe themselves in terms of their jobs, and almost always the secret is poorly kept. Still prevailing but perhaps diminishing today is the practice of identifying women with their husbands' occupations. This is not exclusively an act of male chauvinism because women in their initial meeting frequently will ask, "What does your husband do?" Knowing the answer appears to place women in some sort of "category" so that they can be related to and dealt with.

Rituals unique to a group do develop, but the rituals of the parent culture are likely to be pervasive. In almost every culture, however, there are testing or warm-up rituals which precede almost every meeting. The "how are you?" and "what do you think of the weather?'' remarks seem to be necessary vehicles for leading into more meaningful conversation. These warm-up rituals seem to be more marked at the time of group formation than during the rest of the group's life. However, the ritualistic warm-up is even true, though in lesser degree, at the opening of every session. The symbolic greeting seems needed to help people get acquainted or to renew acquaintance. Some rituals are comfort-seeking devices to make friends or to estab-lish a benign mood for interaction to take place. In a sense the ritual is a reconnaissance such as the process of showing others the deference due.

Symbols also develop in a group. Symbols are part of the action and cannot be separated completely from either ritualis-tic or normative behavior. Looking at these three related processes one might say 1) *rituals* are stylized behavior pat-terns that reflect norms, 2) *symbols* are verbal and visual expressions which communicate the nature of norms and 3) *norms* are the standards which are reflected in ritualistic and symbolic behavior.

Groups develop their own symbolism. In one T-group a rather dignified and aloof executive who wore a jacket and tie even though most other group members dressed informally also treated the group in a rather distant way. As he became more integrated into the group, his manner became more open. He symbolized this difference not by simply changing to the usual informal dress but by donning loud walking shorts and a T-shirt with the slogan "let it all hang out." The group recognized the meaning of this symbolism and cheered him loudly and patted him on the back. In large training labora-tories involving a number of training groups it is not long before group members are sitting together at general sessions and at mealtimes as a symbol of their unity (even when this unity is not manifest in the group).

Expressions that symbolize some dramatic or unusual event in group life are also often incorporated into the special lan-guage of the group. The symbolic language thus developed would be meaningless, even nonsensical, to others, but to the group they are significant. To illustrate, a mental hospital superintendent compared the action of a fellow group member

55

who had been repeating himself to the hospital crew that every week carted a huge grand piano into a recreation hall where patients were engaged in dance therapy. The crew struggled with this monstrous instrument even though all the music for the patients was provided by tape recorder. The superintendent's point was that the restatement of his fellow participant's "hidden agenda" was a useless verbal and intellectual labor. The group had "cracked up" over the superintendent's remark, partially to relieve tension. But each time thereafter when a member recycled an idea or repeated himself someone would say, "Here comes that damned piano again." The piano became a symbol of the group culture and was even portrayed in picture form on the chart pad in the meeting room. Symbolic expressions indicate the progress of a group's socialization process. Expressions such as, "If I read you right," or "Yes, I'm comfortable with that," tend to be repeated over and over as part of the "in" language.

Symbol development accompanies the development of group norms and provides a means of expressing the uniqueness of a particular group. Symbolic interaction is a way in which members communicate to themselves and the group that the norms are understood and that the members are "with it." Using group symbols is a signal of unity and acceptance.

Norms are the standards which serve as guides to group behavior. They are the expectations concerning how the group will operate and how individuals within the group will conduct themselves. Norms govern such things as dress, the type of language used, the way "business" is conducted, the amount of effort expended and outcomes that will be considered satisfactory as joint accomplishment. Norms change or develop as the group develops, and norms are clues to understanding some of the forces that are at work. Norms are products of group interaction and tend to portray the group's progress.

 The group process. Group process includes all of the forces that are operative in groups. In trying to understand group process it is helpful to focus on "special events" as well as concurrent interactions (procedures, substance and feelings), stages of development (dependence, counter-dependence and interdependence) and behavior modes (flight, fight, pairing and work). Group forces are indeed dynamic. Being able to observe, understand and feed back the behaviors as demonstrated in the group process is a major leadership responsibility.

4. Communication In Groups

A name given to one kind of training group is "stranger group," because its members come from several different organizations and disciplines and have never before met. But in a sense almost all groups are stranger groups. Even in organizations where some people see each other almost daily and have worked together for years they know very little about their fellow employees. To a degree urbanization and privatization have occurred simultaneously. Some of the forces of urban life force people into loneliness. Alienation of people from society and estrangement from themselves is a major problem of our time. Although we may nod in a tentative way to the neighbor in the next apartment, talk about work-related activities or engage in small talk with the people with whom we work the interaction we have with others is surprisingly superficial.

The situation is made more clear when people get together in groups. Participants entering the group understand the action only in terms of their private worlds. Unique relationships that will evolve because a particular group of people is addressing a particular set of problems at a specific time are unclear to the participants or maybe unknown. Interpretation of the events will be idiosyncratic, and reaction to these events highly personalized in terms of role perception, invisible committees, personal agendas and stereotypes. For the most part we do not first perceive and then define what we have seen. Rather we see what our private worlds have already defined for us. Our "handy-dandy package" of stereotypes provided by our experiences, cultural norms and values is shifted, re-

59

arranged and sorted so that the situation will appear to conform to our preconceptions (Katz and Kahn, 1966).[1]

Symbolic Private Worlds

A human being's fundamental relation to the world about is a symbolic relation. Action takes place in a person's private world not through a concrete environment, but by the interaction of symbols (Kaplan, 1972).[2] Symbols are the imagery accumulated or created by the person and are the product of that individual's experience.

Burdened or blessed by whatever world they are carrying about our strangers find themselves in an environment which they cannot see clearly and which they do not understand. This environment may provoke feelings of apprehension or comfort. Chairs may be comfortable or not. Noise from the street, elevators or typewriters may make hearing difficult. Strangers must arrange their assortments of stereotypes and symbols, equate these with the environment and find a self-enhancing way to react to what is perceived. Strangers will remain a collection of strangers and will not be a group until portions of their unique worlds are shared with one another and until the strangers become acquaintances or even friends by sharing common experiences.

Common experiences are gained when group members address tasks and interact. As they do so, if the environment is amenable, they become more open with each other.

The Importance of Open Communication

In the exercise of the leadership function there may be no more important task then facilitating open communication. To be open means both to give and to take. Stranger I may attempt to reveal at least some of her private world to the group in the hope that other strangers will also feel safe in doing so. Leadership involves facilitating Stranger I in this process. Stranger I is not only supported, but also helped in learning how to tell others where she is coming from. This process is called *leveling*. It involves examining one's own values, stereotypes and feelings and learning how to explain these to others. Leveling will be of great help to Stranger I in getting acquainted with and learning to like herself.

While others who understand part of what she is saying may feel a bit more comfortable with her the relationship will not improve too much unless more transactions take place. For one thing Stranger I will have to hear what other people are saying. To do this she will have to put her own emotional "baggage" in the "check room" and try to see the world through the eyes of the other strangers who are talking. As she learns to hear with empathy she will begin to hear with understanding. And if she hears what is being communicated, as perceived by the communicators, she will begin to feel more at ease with those persons. The process makes her more respectful and, chances are, more respectable.

With practice group members can begin to understand each other and be understood. When this happens they begin to transact business without the interference of the "noise" caused by factors in the environment or by their own stereotypes.

Unilogues and Dialogues

In the early stages of interaction one can detect a great amount of _unilogue_. The strangers are talking to reassure themselves, to preserve the status quo, to avoid risks. Speech becomes a verbal screen. As the process develops the participation takes on the pattern of _duologues_ in which members lay their ideas, their data, their values and their opinions on others. When they pause for breath or think for a moment others may perceive an opening and jump into the conversation to have their turn. But none among them are burdened with the problem of revealing his or her own values nor with hearing with understanding what is said by others. Arguments start. Polarization occurs. Or maybe worse, boredom sets in.[2]

If groups reach a higher level of effectiveness _dialogue_ begins to take place, and when it does strangers in the group disappear and are replaced by friends and acquaintances. For now people are attempting to level and to hear with understanding. Participants are striving to own their own feelings and to be aware of the feelings of others. Insofar as participants succeed in developing open communication they have acquired the tools for problem solving and effective "work."

The very essence of a social system or organization is the

exchange of information and transmission of meaning. Transformation of energy in the accomplishment of work depends upon communication between people in the group (Katz and Kahn, 1966).[3]

True dialogue cannot take place in a win/lose atmosphere. To win or prevail over me you have to exploit me. For you to succeed under those conditions I must lose. If you are to take advantage of me, even under the rules of the game, you are not likely to be open lest I detect a weakness in you that will thwart you in your purpose. You will tell me only what you want me to hear, and even in the unlikely event I do hear you I will not have all the information I need to interact with you effectively. This will place me at a disadvantage.

Fortunately, in increasing the amount of individual freedom or improving the quality of life it is possible for all participants to be winners. Members of a work team may all succeed and all benefit from the success. Simply stated the process involves the difference between winning an argument and solving a problem. When a problem is solved all involved in the process may be better off; but when some win an argument, this is not so because others must lose.

Communication and the Stage of Group Development

It seems safe to say that adequacy of communication is closely related to conditions of dependence, counter-dependence and interdependence. A dependent situation suggests that the leader or authority person does the initiating and the dependent one complies and responds *in a manner which satisfies the authority person.* Flight behavior would symbolize escape from responsibility and illustrate a desire to keep out of trouble with authority. In a counter-dependent situation the objective would be to fix the blame, to punish, and to win the argument over authority and over other participants. These actions would be calculated to satisfy the counter-dependent person at the expense of others. When interdependence prevails there is an interest in accepting responsibility for one's actions and solving the problem at hand. At the same time one can understand that reaching the solution depends upon being understanding and accepting of the views of others and being willing to work with others. Solving the problem means solving it in a manner satisfactory to all parties of interest. This leads to a *mutually beneficial outcome.*

If communications are the symbol of the act the effort in group development should be to engage in a communications experience which fosters leveling and listening behavior that focuses on problem solving, which in turn leads to energizing the group and enhancing the well-being of all of its members. As a group develops it becomes capable of taking over a great many of the leadership functions, but in an organizational hierarchy the designated leader is required to maintain constant vigilance to fill the leader's role as communications facilitator.

Assume that you are the leader of this group of 12 strangers. (It could be a training group, project team, task force, work unit or almost any collection of people brought together to work to some purpose.) As leader you hope to facilitate the release of each individual's energy for the purpose of achieving individual and group goals. Knowing the group is faced with a good bit of ambiguity and apprehension you expect dependent behavior. You know that the only way that a team will finally come together is by sharing experiences and building trust. You have convened the group, letting them know to the best of your ability the general nature of the task with which the group is charged and the limits that may be placed on the group's freedom to act (area of freedom). You also have suggested the initial procedures calculated to start the interaction process within the group.

You, of course, are aware that by the very fact of opening the meeting and making your initial orientation presentation that you have reinforced the dependency relationship between you and the group. In the members' eyes you are more responsible than they. Now you are through with the orientation and your hope is that the group will take over the task of exploring the problem. You indicate this and wait expectantly for group members to go to work. For an interminable 33 seconds they sit looking at you. Finally someone speaks. But the person speaking does not address the task, but rather asks you to "clarify" what you have said. This individual is joined by others who also ask you questions. Most of these are "non-questions" asked to confirm preconceptions, to subtly cast doubt on what you have said or to imply the group is really powerless to accomplish the mission you have indicated. These questions will mostly be telling you that the group wishes more guidance. The members are saying, "Please don't put us to work on our own."

The Question Trap

You do not answer the questions but say that it is up to the group to determine the answers. In fits and starts the members begin to direct their conversations toward each other, but most of them will be looking at you as they talk. Others may generally address the group but glance at you frequently to see if they "are doing all right." The furtive glance at the designated leader is a non-verbal cue indicating member dependency. Some members will continue by these glances to check on leader approval until very late in the process of group development. If in addition to being group leader you are the boss of the persons in the group the urge to "keep an eye on you" may be a permanent adjunct of some of the dependent members' behavior. This is also unilogue time. Listening to a taped segment of a group conversation would enable one to note a series of virtually unconnected statements, with each speaker developing a separate theme. Some people interrupt, and in a vital and lively group sometimes two or three people are talking at one time—still, mind you, attempting to obtain your attention because you are the leader.

Since you have purposely taken yourself out of the interaction you are able to observe that one or two participants are taking all the "air time" while others are silent. Some of the silent ones are listening with non-verbal signs of agitation. One or two members may appear to be lost in their own thoughts. As the group continues to unfold each individual begins to establish his or her pattern of participation. In almost any group some persons are quite verbal, while others are relatively silent. Some silent types participate actively by listening but need to be assisted when, by non-verbal signs, they show they are finally ready to speak. One of the leadership tasks is to be aware of the signals being sent by the members of the group. Often the less verbal hesitate to jump in because by doing so they would appear to be interrupting. Stranger II in our group may have started actively throwing out ideas which the group ignored by going on to other topics as soon as this member had finished. Or worse still Stranger II's comments may have been greeted with silence. Incensed at this Stranger II withdraws and sulks even pushing his or her chair back out of the circle a foot or two.

The Seduction Trap

You also note that Stranger III, who has been only moderately active during the session, corners you as the meeting breaks up and gives you his or her ideas as to what is wrong with the group. Later he or she is likely to have good advice for you, the leader, and also will make some comments on the behavior of the other group members. Apparently he or she expects you to intercede in the group as agent and protector. You gently suggest that it might be a good idea for Stranger III to bring his or her own comments to the attention of the group for their reaction. Stranger III's efforts at lobbying are not unusual in the group and unfortunately entrap or seduce some leaders who become anxious when the group engages in "irresponsible" behavior, and therefore welcome an opportunity to tell some sympathetic person like Stranger III that this mess is really not the leader's fault (Thelen, 1954).[4]

Scapegoating

But you know better. You avoided the question trap and the seduction trap, but, of course, there are a number of other difficulties which confront you. Another trap is becoming fascinated with and engaging in the group's normal penchant for "scapegoating." For even strangers can unite on a mutual hate object, castigating and belaboring people and causes which they agree are abhorrent. Frequently these scapegoat objects are outside the group, making the attack doubly safe. But the activity can occur within the group as well. Here the unwary leader may derive a sufficient degree of satisfaction to join in the fun. (After all, the group is misbehaving and some of the miscreants deserve punishment.) But you have not joined the hunting pack nor have you tried to protect the quarry. Your role, if the timing seems right, is to suggest that people pause and take a look at what is happening. If they can talk about the scapegoating they will have learned a valuable lesson. But in the early stages of group life the strangers may ignore your suggestion. At least by making the suggestion you have done no harm.

Another reason for avoiding participation in the "scapegoating" action is the general need for the leader to avoid partisan emotional involvement in group activity. If the leader does so become involved the leader may lose touch with unfolding events and even become part of the problem. When criticized or attacked, leaders should work hard at hearing what is said rather than attempting to defend or explain their positions. Leaders should avoid contesting with group members even though participants exercise great energy and ingenuity in attempting to get leaders to do so. Leaders can also avoid the oracle role. Group members vest the leader with such a role by the stereotype they carry about concerning leadership behavior.

People as Things

It is almost standard practice that as participants begin to discuss the ideas and behaviors of others in the group they do so as if these other participants were unfeeling objects or perhaps not even present in the room. In this case the leader might suggest experimenting with talking to rather than about the other person. The participant exchange which would cause your intervention might resemble this:

Al: "You know I didn't understand why Mary seemed provoked when Larry told her she was easier to deal with than most women."

Mary is sitting across the circle from Al at the time but you would not think that Al knew this since he is making his remarks mostly to the leader. If the leader were successful in convincing Al he should talk to Mary then Al might say,

"Mary, I don't understand why you got upset when Larry said you were easier to deal with than most women."

In the discussion of forces at work in groups we have mentioned that people sometimes fall into flight, fight and pairing behavior patterns. These patterns are naturally manifest in verbal and non-verbal behavior. Fliers will divert attention away from conflict or work by introducing extraneous, irrelevant or untimely subjects. They will "leave" the group by retreating to the inner sanctum of their private worlds, by walking around the room or engaging in some other physical diversion, or even in their most hostile moments by reading a newspaper or doing other extraneous "work" while the meeting is in session. Flight ingenuity knows few bounds, but the many ways in which this type of communication occurs is recognizable by its diversionary or escape characteristics. Fliers delight in the "there and then" and are inclined to be verbally active when the group is engaging in avoidance behavior.

Fighters tend to find these moments boring. They may sit on the sidelines in amused silence, or they may be downright disgusted. As one would expect this mood is discernible in the fighter's non-verbal behavior. In general the cues fighters transmit are hostile: they sulk rather than talk, enduring the process in silence; they sit on the sidelines, bored and smouldering. Let a fight start and these people lean forward and may even pull their chairs forward a bit and spring into the fray. Groups spurred on by fighters may take advantage of persons who are attempting to reveal their values, beliefs and problems by playing district attorney.

Fighters particularly are fascinated with the opportunity to bore in with probing questions. Sometimes the rasping nature of their questions creates anger or discomfort. This worries the fliers who may first try to ameliorate, and if they are not successful to withdraw. Fliers may seek safety by pairing. Pairing permits them to avoid the larger conflict and seek refuge by aligning themselves with friendly neighbors. Pairing may be the refuge of fliers and a weapon of the fighters (who will use the pairing association to disrupt and attack the group). As noted previously some people who do not seem to be committed as either fliers or fighters pair because group activity is out of phase with their private world. True, they may be stimulated by some occurrence in the group, but they need to pursue the idea so stimulated in a setting which they more nearly control and which is not subject to the larger group.

As an experienced and perceptive leader you will recognize the difference between casual and intermittent pairing and the kind of pairing that breaks up the group faced with a troublesome dilemma or tension due to conflict. When a group disintegrates through pairing, the process deserves to be examined. The leader can often facilitate group understanding by helping members look at what is occurring during the moments when disintegration due to pairing takes place.

As the leader you have thus far communicated in several ways:

1) letting participants know what you and they are expected to accomplish,

2) setting up procedures which enable participants to voice their expectations,

3) facilitating movement toward reconciliation of the participants' expectations with the mission or charge,

4) helping participants to help themselves in efforts to agree on the agenda and

5) modeling facilitative leadership behavior which includes listening, leveling and encouraging process observation.

As a result of your effort to break the dependency chain and to be accepting of counter-dependent behavior group members will accuse you of engaging in avoidance and manipulative activities. Some will say you are playing games with them. But you have told the group members that they must shape their own destiny and have noted that you would neither give them a road map nor respond to their blandishments. Your role has been one of facilitating communication, helping in skill development and suggesting procedures (which the group may accept or reject) for gaining mutual experience. In other words your interaction with the group members has been designed to

help them do what they wish to do while you avoided authoritarian behavior which would interfere with individual and
group growth.

Modeling by the Leader

One of your major contributions has been to provide the
group members with a model for giving each other feedback.
You have shown that the effective way to provide feedback is
to talk about what has actually happened, what has been observed or how you feel, not what the person's intentions were
in carrying out the act. You made it clear that there is no way
that one individual can know another's intentions. If a person
backs his chair out of the circle you do not say that person is
counter-dependent or flying—the feedback notes that the chair
is pushed back out of the circle and the person is given an
opportunity to interpret his or her own actions (Lehner,
1974).[5]

Communication processes are the vehicles which make group
development possible when the leadership in the group oper-
ates within the general concepts of Maslow, McGregor and
Lewin. If the leader understands the forces at work in groups
the leader can assist group members to understand role, operate within the framework of effective learning theory and
demonstrate the value of the self-management orientation.

5. Methodology

Group leadership involves using a wide variety of training methods from lecturettes to free discussion and from audio-visual presentations to group games. Success of an endeavor may be helped by sensitive application of the appropriate method at the right time. Unfortunately it is not true that given good people you can forget the methodology. The method employed is important. *How* the method is employed is vital. While a number of the methods discussed here may be applied in authoritarian and manipulative ways, they are likely to fail under such circumstances. Assumptions which influence the leadership mode will reveal themselves in the manner in which these methods are applied. Here is a list of assumptions which seem pertinent to effective democratic leadership:

1) Every individual has worth as a person and is entitled to maintain his or her self-respect and dignity.

2) Human beings have a capacity to learn and grow as a result of new emotional-intellectual experiences.

3) The learning most apt to influence attitudes and behavior comes about by having procedural, substantive and emotional experiences and then reflecting upon them.

4) A democratic group climate conducive to free discussion and experimentation with different ways of operating and behaving is a necessary condition for learning.

5) The leadership role carries responsibility for helping participants learn from their experiences. This involves

facilitating the development of an open and energy releasing atmosphere and the willingness to encourage scrutiny of the leader's own behavior.

6) The most democratic way to work is to share in the diagnosis of problems and to plan and evaluate activities collaboratively.

7) The study of the group process helps improve group efficiency and productivity (Nylan, Mitchel and Stout, n.d.).[1]

Given the psychologically handicapped nature of a people conditioned by an hierarchical culture the leader should strive to help the group develop the environment, the skills and the psychological competence needed to move toward democratic forms of organizational behavior. This does not mean that the leader cannot share information, suggest approaches to problem solving, give feedback and encourage others to give and receive feedback, introduce procedures which facilitate group process or be an open and caring person. Leaders need to take a pro-active and influencing role, but the thrust of these actions should be power diffusing and helpful to the self-enhancing processes of the individual, organization and society. More specifically under the pro-active approach the methodology is selected within the following context:

1) The approach creates situations which bring about the development of a learning community in which participants learn from each other and teach each other, and where the leaders also engage as full participants in the learning and teaching process.

2) Leaders establish a model for behavior by their participation, acceptance of criticism, non-evaluative comments, willingness to deviate from pre-planned procedures, ability to listen with understanding, ability to capture and reflect feelings, by their clarifying comments and by the method of expressing their own feelings.

3) By example the leaders explicitly or implicitly introduce democratic values to the group. They do this by the way in which they focus attention on problems in order to stimulate group awareness and by their willingness to relinquish the position of authority and leadership to the group.

72

4) Leaders facilitate the flow of communication by clarifying issues and encouraging full participation of group members toward development of mutual understanding. Because of being less personally involved leaders can help bring about recognition and potential solution to problems when sources of difficulty are below the level of awareness of group members.

5) Leaders participate by introducing knowledge derived from their experience or from research findings which the group may desire and need in order to solve a given problem. This must be done with integrity and skill so that the leader is diminishing or avoiding the "expert" role (Tannenbaum, Weschler and Massarik, 1970).[2]

Within these stated assumptions the leader has a wide range of development approaches available. Most of these take the action training and research approach in which participants survey the situation, agree on the problems, experiment with possible solutions and evaluate results. It should be helpful to the developing group leader to 1) understand the nature of broad development approaches—for example, the learning community, action training and research, organization development, management by objectives, transactional analysis and the Blake grid; 2) examine some rather specific methodology which might be employed in group sessions; 3) discuss some of the options available to the leader in certain recurring group situations; 4) become able to use audio-visual materials that enhance operations of the learning community; and 5) engage in some straight talk about logistics and how to avoid letting the "little things" kill you.

It is useful for those interested in group leadership to be aware of the richness of the various ways in which organizations are going about the business of group development. There are a number of major developmental approaches, some of which come close to being sub-disciplines in the major development field. The literature on groups deals with many of these in some depth and therefore in the last section this monograph will provide bibliographic notes on the more significant work which pertains to major development approaches. One quickly emerging notion relates to the development of a "working community."

Developing A Working Community

Members of a staff, task force or training group are likely to work more productively if leaders can stimulate the development of a sense of community. Development of the sense of community starts with a "declaration of faith" or a statement of expectations by both the participants and the sponsoring organization. Synergyzing the wants of the individual and the organization becomes an early problem solving activity. Parties engage in consultation concerning their aspirations with the express purpose of "getting what everyone wants." In other words everyone will win. Thus the individual develops the unique program that suits his or her purpose while the organization emerges with a total program intended to accomplish its end. In such learning or work communities the ideal is to foster both self-management and collaborative effort so that: 1) every worker is a boss and every boss a worker, 2) every learner is a teacher and every teacher a learner.

The National Training and Development Service (NTDS) has been attempting to develop a learning/working community in the context of its summer programs. The work in these programs is illustrative of the process which may be adapted to any work unit in most major jurisdictions.

Element No. 1. The first element in the NTDS process is *preparation*. NTDS is interested in action training and research as a major strategy for dealing with change in state and local government. So the NTDS preparation involves making arrangements with a "laboratory community" which will provide a locale where session participants can practice and learn action training and research skills in an actual operating situation.

NTDS also prepares and sends to prospective participants an outline of tasks to be completed before persons attend the program. In the same brochure NTDS outlines its general expectations as to the outcomes it deserves as its part of the "contract." Then prospective participants, with some knowledge of the nature of the NTDS Training of Training and Development Managers' program, have an opportunity to decide if the proposed program appears to meet their needs.

74

They have an opportunity at this time to decide whether or not to attend. If the answer is affirmative participants are asked to undertake five major tasks to prepare themselves for the four-week program. The first task is to assess their own strengths and weaknesses as an individual and to determine "where" they wish to be in five years. The second task is to collect data on their own organization's strength, weakness and possibilities for change. In task three the participants collect information on the social environment in which their organizations operate. In task four, individuals have an opportunity to develop personal learning designs based upon the data collected in tasks 1, 2 and 3, which they would hope to complete during the seminar. The final task is to develop information on a particular problem participants wish to work on during the four-week seminar. This problem should be amenable to the action training and research process.

This data collection and program planning are part of the preparation because of the NTDS desires to direct seminar learning toward reality-based problems.

To stimulate further participants, concern over their own learning NTDS asks attendees to complete a questionnaire intended to reflect their personal training interests. This questionnaire has been developed through the course of several seminars. Information secured from composite responses enables the NTDS staff to prepare and accumulate materials which may be needed to meet the express needs of participants.

The pre-seminar activities are all part of the data-gathering element which is intended to accelerate community building. NTDS's theory is that a community is derived from the collaboration of community members who share the perception that their wants can best be met by helping and by being helped. A community begins to develop when members have some idea as to the nature of their own wants and the degree to which these wants provide a common ground for working with others. Given the commonality of wants there is a natural desire to discover who can help fulfill the wants. All the information developed in the pre-seminar preparation state is reproduced and disseminated to participants.

Element No. 2 — Skills inventory. It follows that when prospective community members have made an exploration of their own needs and wants they develop another need which is to take stock of the resources available within the learning and work community provided by the seminar. So when the session begins NTDS provides information on staff background and skills. Also participants engage very early in an interviewing exercise, one purpose of which is to derive and record information on the wide range of talent which members bring to the group. As with the pre-seminar work data developed in these interviews are reproduced and distributed to all community members. Part of the community building process is gathering and sharing information which has validity in the eyes of participants. It has this validity because it has been collected, studied and tested in a shared effort. The data then have value because those who develop the data have invested themselves in the collection.

Element No. 3. The third element is based on agreeing upon a *work and learning contract*. Participation in contract development is a problem solving activity involving three questions:

1) What wants of mine do I expect to have met by the community?

2) What do I expect to do that will help meet the wants of the community (including the wants of NTDS)?

3) What assistance do I expect from the NTDS staff?

While the expectations of NTDS have been provided to participants in advance these are re-stated at the contract building juncture so that participants will be familiar with NTDS wants. Participants produce individual contract proposals which are examined by the group. An effort is made to provide means of meeting all wants. If sufficient talent and resources do not exist then this deficiency is openly examined. Individuals revise their proposals on the basis of the group examination. Then they and staff conclude agreements and develop schedules for meeting contract terms. Concluding the contract assists the community development process by improving communications between members, thus enriching common (community) perceptions. Contracts are also declarations of intent. Participants will feel responsibility to meet the terms of the contract to the degree they have developed these agreements with serious intent. The degree of intentionality is directly connected with the strength of the driving force for community solidarity. Also as group norms develop for successful contract implementation the cohesiveness of the community should tend to increase.

Element No. 4. Both staff and participants as community members go about fulfilling the terms of their contracts. The *work* in the NTDS seminar has to do with developing training skills and knowledge about training as a management strategy plus engaging in and learning about an action training and research project that involves a pressing problem in a real public agency. All of these activities can, if carried out within a framework of democratic values, provide for an increased interdependence among community members. Much of the training emphasizes improvement of communication skills. As community members teach each other, there is an increase in knowledge and a sharpening of interpersonal skills, particularly among those who invest heavily in teaching roles.

Element No. 5 — Evaluation. From time to time, but at least at the conclusion of any milestone noting the completion of a contract the community pauses for process observation. At first this inward look is modeled by staff. Very soon, however, community members accept the responsibility. In the process observation activity members learn to give feedback on observable behavior and upon their own feelings about what is happening (Lehner, 1974).[3] They compare the targets stated in the contract with events as they have actually occurred. Community members are goal-oriented just as are other members of society, but community members have both the vehicle and the incentive to take the time necessary to check progress. Under these conditions commitment to achievement tends to run quite high.

Element No. 6 — Recycling. In the process of contract implementation and evaluation new realities emerge. Estimated situations turn out to be different, at least in degree, from those that were expected. Changes might have occurred in the environment. Aspiration might turn out to be too high or too low, and the capability of community members might have been higher or lower than anticipated. All evaluations are grist for the mill. Here, as at every step, self-management and group decision are the method by which the community is governed.

Work communities appear to be subject to the same group forces as are other continuing groups; and when an interdependent stage is reached the learning or working community has been established. Efforts made by NTDS have contributed a great deal of knowledge on how to make working communities operational. It seems safe to say that the process now utilized by NTDS is applicable to any *containable* work unit or work project. By perceptive use of the six community building elements a great deal can be done to establish a sense of community in an operational setting.

Another change process involves the methodologies of Action Training and Research.

Action Training and Research

Action research is research that is diagnostic, involves as participants those persons who will be affected by research outcomes, is sometimes but not always empirical, is experimental and as a result of its conscious problem solving thrust leads to commitment and acceptable action.

Action training is training specifically designed to help those with the declared responsibility for a given action to comprehend and translate program concepts into reality.

Action research is essentially a method of sensing the internal and external environments of an organization or community; of deciding whether problems exist; and if there are problems, if they are worthy of expending time and energy to resolve. If the level of tension is sufficient the process calls for spelling out the aspiration of those involved in analyzing restraining and driving forces and then experimenting with the action options available in tentative time-limited ways which might bring about solutions to the problems. By assisting in collecting the data, defining the problem and experimenting with possible solutions people learn and change. Action research is a normative-re-educative approach to change (Gardner, 1973).[4] If experiments are successful then a program is designed to which the organization can commit itself and program implementation takes place. At the same time the process for evaluation and feedback is instituted to keep the program from growing old. The process should always be thought of as continuing, carrying with it the necessity for recycling at agreed upon times. By planning for recycling, organization renewal becomes a continuing process and may even become a way of life.

Training traditionally attempts to convey general skills and knowledge that help people become better managers, more knowledgeable budget officers, faster readers or improved letter writers. Action training on the other hand is designed to give people particular skills and knowledge to execute specific jobs and responsibilities within a foreseeable time span. It is used as a means of converting new policies and new programs into services delivered. Action training calls for:

1) focusing on objectives;

2) developing an understanding of the context in which the proposed action is to take place;

3) either overcoming the resistance to the proposed action by developing an understanding of the change itself and the reasons behind it; or, failing this, influencing the elimination or modification of the proposed action; and

4) helping persons who have implementation responsibility to acquire knowledge and skills needed to be effective in the implementation process.

Action training is a necessary accompaniment to action research because only through training can people comprehend and develop know-how to participate in a meaningful and effective manner in the self-searching activity. There are still many administrators who do not seem to understand the importance of training as an implementation tool. Action training is an administrative strategy that when competently used is equally important as budgeting and personnel processes as an implementation and change strategy. Action training represents a relatively untouched method for enhancing the quality, credibility, execution and acceptance of new policies and programs.

Organization development, which is an over-arching method-ology with many elements akin to action research and training, also offers a rich resource to those interested in solving people problems (Gardner, 1973).[5]

Organization Development

Organization Development (OD) is "a complex educational strategy intended to change beliefs, attitudes, values and structures so that they can better adapt" to new technologies and challenges (Bennis, 1969).[6]

As it has come to be practiced OD generally takes place in a group setting. At times there may be multiple groups involved with several areas or hierarchical levels participating. A con-sultant acts as group facilitator to help the group work through an educational process that is intended to stimulate change. Changes sought are those which the group itself sees as being desirable. Consultants use many of the methods noted here to assist the group in examining its problems. In most OD pro-grams the consultant helps group members 1) generate data relating to the problems being examined, 2) feed back data to relevant decision makers and implementors and 3) plan action based on the group's findings (Gardner, 1969).[7]

Top executives in development programs are prepared for OD programs in their own organizations by attending "stranger laboratories" where they participate in a T-group with execu-tives from other organizations. (National Training Laboratories conduct several such groups each year. On the West Coast UCLA has one laboratory each year especially designed for public executives and two other group sessions which invite managers from both public and private sectors as participants.) With top management having some sense of the process in-volved OD sessions are conducted within the organization. The top manager is by now aware of the process and begins to understand the foment and the development that is occurring with each group being trained.

Many organizations now use team building as the major element of their OD programs. In team building the actual work team meets together periodically to examine the unit's liability in regard to human satisfaction, development in the team, interpersonal conflict within the group and organizational effectiveness. In most team building sessions consultants try to help groups develop action steps for future behavior.

There are other types of groups limited it seems only by organizational needs and the ingenuity of the OD consultant involved. Sometimes two work units face the need for cooperation on a project or for resolution of differences. Managers from the two units are brought together, usually in a retreat location away from the job and with the help of a consultant attempt to resolve the issues. At other times groups are made up from a cross-section of managers belonging to the same organizational level in the hierarchy. This type of session is frequently referred to as a "cousin" group.

Whatever the type of group or the specific nature of the subject matter most group effort reflects the normative goals of increased interpersonal competence, resolution of group tensions, better communications, a higher level of authenticity and trust, organic rather than mechanistic problem solving and more effective team management (Gardner, 1969).[8] OD carries with it the implicit value of collaborative management. Most behavioral science interventions, including OD strategies are interventions that when successful, reenforce tendencies toward diffusion of power (Blake and Mouton, 1971).[9]

OD is not a one-time thing but a continuing organizational effort. Many organizations use both inside and outside consultants in OD activities. Outside consultants need not be socialized by organizational norms; when they are not, they can provide an independent point of view. Internal consultants on the other hand could be expected to become better acquainted with the problems and folklore of the organizations for which they work. Together the inside and outside consultants can assist in nurturing a continuing program which can help an organization in its efforts to humanize itself.

Socio-Technical Systems

Socio-technical systems call for the use of change strategies to develop organizational environments compatible with both

the social and technical needs of persons in the client organization. Investigators with the Tavistock Institute who conduct
socio-technical system studies believe that the following
psychological requirements are present in most types of work
and should serve as a basis for developing jobs from tasks:

1) the need for the content of the duties of the position to be
reasonably demanding in terms other than sheer endurance,

2) the need for being able to learn on the job and to go on
learning (but not too much or too little),

3) the need for some area of decision making that attaches to
the individual,

4) the need for social support and recognition in the work
place,

5) the need for the individual to relate what is done at work
to the social processes of life and

6) the need to feel that the job leads to some sort of desirable
future (Emery and Trist, 1965).[10]

"The efforts in the socio-tech approach are applied to help
the client institution's productive efforts 1) meet environmental requirements, 2) meet the changes in the environment
which may be induced by the institution and 3) become sensitive to changes independently taking place in the environment. In working to achieve a pro-active interrelationship in
turbulent fields the socio-tech approach concerns itself with
people, the organization and the environment while giving
great attention to values which are the persistent response to a
milieu of relative uncertainty." (Emery and Trist, 1970).[11]

"The socio-technical system strategy provides another compatible approach to dealing with changing." Its values are
democratic and supportive of the consent element inherent in
popular sovereignty (Gardner, 1973).[12]

Still another methodological construct is Management by
Objectives.

Management by Objectives (MBO)

There are many approaches to MBO but the approach which elicits genuine participation of the employee in determining and accepting responsibility and benefits for his work unit within the legal constraints and values of the larger organization is a valuable normative-reeducative strategy of changing (Drucker, 1954).[13] "The basic concepts embodied in MBO can be summarized as follows:

1) The objectives (explicit expected results to be accomplished) are diverse and multi-dimensional.

2) In order to be useful the objectives need to be understood by persons designated to achieve them.

3) Objectives developed by persons who are to achieve them are likely to be more acceptable and have greater utility than those developed for them by management.

4) Organizations must take cognizance of goals and objectives of the individual so that *integration* of those goals and objectives supplants differentiation of such goals and objectives.

5) Statements of objectives are of little use unless they enable the organization to determine whether or not the desired result has been achieved in the time specified. When objectives are so conceived they may be considered as operating objectives.

6) Operating objectives are inadequate if they do not permit the development of a schedule of events which communicates progress toward achievement of results.

7) Objectives should meet the needs of individuals and organizations for both immediate and deferred gratification, if possible, but in any case the former should not supersede the latter.

8) Individual responsibility for achievement of objectives should be a matter of specific understanding.

9) Once objectives have been accomplished resources should be re-oriented and be re-grouped toward achievement of other organization and individual objectives, which should

in turn strive for ethical, psychological, social and material improvements" (Gardner, 1972).[14]

"An underlying value which attaches to MBO is that 'man will exercise self-direction and self-control in the service of objectives to which he is committed.' " (McGregor, 1960)[15]

"It should be clear by now that the normative-reeducative strategies proposed in this paper strongly suggests that institutions are open systems, changing in nature, constantly interacting with social, technical and organizational environments." (Gardner, 1973)[16]

Another over-arching methodology involving groups and the group processes is Transactional Analysis.

Transactional Analysis (TA)

Transactional analysis is based on the notion that the unit of social intercourse is the transaction. A transaction includes a transactional stimulus and transactional response. "Simple transaction analysis is concerned with diagnosing which ego state implemented the transactional stimulus and which one executed the transactional response." (Berne, 1964)[17]

Transactional analysis practitoners claim to have found a new language of psychology which moves us closer to the secret of human behavior than we have ever been before (Harris, 1967).[18] Central to the TA language is the definition given to Parent, Adult and Child. These three states, they say, exist in all grown people.

Parent. In each grown person there is a perpetual Parent who is a "tape recording" of the behavior of the person's own parents. This recording is full of rages, admonitions, cooing or praise. Likewise the tape has such items as "never tell a lie," "clean your plate," "never trust a woman (or man)" and "busy hands are happy hands." Whether or not the information on these tapes is reasonable it comes through to the person who is carrying it around as "truth." Throughout a person's life he will replay this tape when his Parent is showing, and at these moments the behavior that results is likely to be coercing, manipulative, forcing, restrictive or sometimes permissive

(Harris, 1967).[19] Harris says that we may think of the Parent as generally representing the transaction between that person's two parents—sort of stereophonic. If the two parents harmonize, great; if they do not the Parent as a whole is weakened and productive of anxiety.

Adult. At about ten months a child finds it is able to act out of its own awareness and original thought. Self-actualization is beginning and the first signs of the Adult show. In the early years the Adult in us is minimal. But with growth the Adult in us becomes stronger. In the Adult mode one is principally concerned with transforming stimuli into information which can be understood and acted upon in terms of past experience (Berne, 1961).[20] Adult action will test Parent data. If parental instruction is reality based the Adult will come to recognize its integrity (Harris, 1967).[21] Parent data are updated through validation by the Adult; reaction of the Child is to determine what behavior is safe under the circumstances.

In TA the hypothesis is that the Adult in us can be recognized, and when this occurs can be nourished and will grow.

Child. The Child provides the "want to" part of an individual. When the Child sees a reality that conflicts with its experience, the child is likely to accept the verdict of what it has been told rather than to rely on experience. "For a little child it may be safer to believe a lie than to believe his own eyes and ears." (Harris, 1967)[22] The outcome of the socializing process is a development of negative feelings. Children are forced to see themselves as "not O.K."

Transactional analysts tend to believe there are four major ways in which persons may look at themselves.

Four Life Positions. Transactional analysts talk about these four life positions relating to interpersonal transactions:

1) I'm not O.K.—You're O.K.

2) I'm not O.K.—You're not O.K.

3) I'm O.K.—You're not O.K.

4) I'm O.K.—You're O.K.

The universal position of early childhood and the one into

which we revert when the Child within us is controlling our behavior is "I'm not O.K. – You're O.K." Most of the evidence a child receives from others and from its small size and helplessness is that it is inferior. This mode becomes the person's life script. (T.A. people involve participants in "script" analysis, a script being a person's perception of how life should be lived.) The Child in us may try to behave in a way to obtain "strokes" (approval and reward indicating "that's a good child").

Stroking generally continues from time to time during a child's first year, but as mobility and self-sufficiency develop the situation may lead to abandonment of stroking or less interest being shown in the individual by others. No longer is the preoccupation with getting strokes paying off for the child. This leads to a feeling of "I'm not O.K. – You're not O.K." If this position becomes firm a child even rejects stroking. It is a difficult position to change once it is thoroughly incorporated into "self." If a child is brutalized she or he may come to believe "I'm O.K. – You're not O.K." In this case the individual has learned to administer strokes to self. After growing up this person acts "without conscience," is in extreme cases capable of justifying homicide and rejects the strokes of others because their strokes are not worth having.

While these three positions, I' not O.K. – You're O.K., I'm not O.K. – You're not O.K., and I'm O.K. – You're not O.K., are based on feelings and are unconscious the fourth, I'm O.K. – You're O.K., is based on thought, faith and conscious decision.

In TA training is directed to cause and effect of transactions between Child and Parent, Child and Adult, Child and Child, Parent and Child, Parent and Adult, Parent and Parent, Adult and Child, Adult and Adult, and Adult and Parent. By recognition of behavior one may practice and learn Adult behavior.

The implications are that:

1) everyone has parents and carries with him ego states that reflect the ego states of Parent,

2) every individual can learn objective data processing if that person attains an appropriate ego state and

3) everyone carries fixated perceptions from other years that can be activated under certain conditions (Berne, 1961).[23]

TA is utilized by a number of organizations as a development vehicle. As is the case with general systems concepts TA provides symbolic and abstract means of analyzing human interaction and behavior.

Another type of group that has become more common in the last few years is the Gestalt group.

Gestalt Groups.

Fritz Perls sought a name for the therapeutic approach he was developing, and since he had been profoundly influenced by the German psychological school of Gestalt he labeled his groups Gestalt groups (Levitsky and Simkin, 1972).[24]

Gestalt groups are comprised of from five to eight participants often meeting in weekly meetings that run from one and a half to three hours. Sessions are intensely leader-centered, and much of the action occurs between the leader and a single member. In a sense this is a case of individual therapy taking place in front of the group. But the activities of Gestalt leaders are not standardized. "Any particular set of techniques, such as our presently used rules and games, will be regarded merely as convenient means—whereby useful tools for our purposes have no sacrosanct qualities." (Levitsky and Perls, 1970)[25] Gestaltists point out that though they firmly control procedures and interaction processes their stance is not authoritarian because they do not tell participants how to conduct their lives.

The underlying concern of Gestaltists is with the totality of functioning since they are convinced that the problem of life is to make it livable. This entails recognition that one's finiteness leads to anxiety. The aim is not to eliminate anxiety but to accept that it is part of the nature of things. The Gestalt approach is a prepared quest for authenticity (Levitsky and Simkin, 1972).[26]

Some well-trained group leaders are able to employ Gestalt approaches in other types of group sessions. Since Gestalt groups are leader-directed there is a possibility that the approach can interfere with processes geared to group rather than individual development. With its leader-centeredness it has the potential of maintaining groups in the dependent state. Some Gestaltists are experimenting with means of combining group dynamics and Gestalt approaches.

In the meantime organizations finding places for appropriate use of Gestalt methods would do well to examine the credentials of the leaders they employ. Utilizing Gestalt methodology calls for careful theoretical and practical training. Such groups are no place for amateur leaders. Gestalt groups are intensely personal. A group methodology which approaches development in a more impersonal way (although it can involve the development of insight and personalized learning) is the instrumented laboratory.

Instrumented Learning

Instrumented learning is a term applied to a development process that utilizes carefully designed instruments to provide feedback to group participants and generate data for discussion and growth. We will describe the *Managerial Grid* as illustrative of the instrumented approach since it is perhaps the most well-known "package" of instrumented learning. At the same time you should know that there are other, less publicized approaches which are useful when employed under appropriate conditions.

Robert S. Blake and Jane Srygley Mouton describe their concepts of instrumented learning in their book, *The Managerial Grid* (Blake and Mouton, 1964).[27] Central to the process is a self-assessment instrument to determine managerial orientations. The instrument touches the factors of 1) decisions, 2) convictions, 3) conflict, 4) emotions (temper), 5) humor and 6) effort. After the instrument is completed answers of individuals are scored and categorized as falling within one of the following dimensions:

1) Concern for production. This is the degree of concern which is present in the boss toward production as may be seen in policy decisions, the number of creative ideas that applied research turns into useful activity, procedures or processes and other actions that are not necessarily related to things. Its proper meaning covers those things that organizations attempt to accomplish.

2) Concern for people. Included in this is the concern for the degree of personal commitment for the persons completing a job for which the individual feels responsible, trust rather than obedience, self-esteem or consideration of the personal worth of an individual, establishing and maintaining good working conditions and concern over the maintenance of fair salary structures, security for employees and social relationships with associates (Blake and Mouton, 1964).[28]

It is the purpose of the Grid to depict ways and assumptions about how an individual can manage. The instrument develops a picture of the dominant style of an individual. After individuals complete the instrument the results are posted in "Grid form" from which is derived the name Managerial Grid. The Grid is formed on two axes with the horizontal axis depicting the concern for production and the vertical axis the concern for people. Thus in the lower lefthand corner one would find a low concern for people and a low concern for production. (One might describe university administration as being a pure example of 1/1 management.) In the lower righthand corner one would find 9/1 management, with a very high concern for production with little regard for the people. The upper lefthand corner of the Grid would show 1/9, a high concern for people but little attention being given to work accomplishment. "The ideal" is shown in the upper righthand corner of the Grid by 9/9 management in which we find an "interdependent" organizational state with concern for both people and product.

Blake and Mouton say that a manager's place on the grid indicates an "anchorage" for managerial aptitudes and practices. They believe that the grid describes systems of pressures which compel an individual to manage in a certain fashion. In their view these pressures arise from inside the person, from the immediate external situation or from the characteristics of the organizational system including traditions, practices and procedures.

What we have been discussing are a number of methodological constructs which provide a framework within which individual group processes can be invoked. While these are useful persons who are developing as group leaders will also need more specific, technique-oriented methods. It is noted that these various techniques can be utilized in a variety of groups which cut across some of the philosophical lines represented by the overarching methods we have just described.

6. Group Leadership Methods
(Gardner, 1969)[1]

The leader bears a great burden in regard to facilitating group effort. Desirable attributes of the training group leader are also desirable attributes for the team leader in program work groups. In most cases as we have stressed the leader is a coordinator and a facilitator. The leader attempts to help a group learn how to protect itself and its individual members from the tyranny of authority from whatever direction it might come. The leader must have great faith and trust in the capacities of the group. In those cases where the leader takes unilateral procedural action he or she must do so in a way that permits challenge and alteration if the group or individual involved takes exception to this action.

Usually the time available for the deliberations is not sufficient to take care of all organizational needs. For this reason the leader probably should assume that his or her position has delegated to it the responsibility for intervening in interpersonal emergencies as well as in procedural and substantive areas which have been approved in principle by team members. Team members are given an atmosphere in which they develop norms in a way that fosters the kind of understanding which permits great freedom of activity compatible with group beliefs. Within the understood (formalized or unformalized) power delegated to him or her by the work group the leader should feel free to go ahead and take necessary action to keep the work of the group moving toward objectives. In so doing the leader should sense that the group members are "with him" and would endorse his action if time permitted the group to consider the problems with which the leader is faced. In those instances where the leader feels the group is divided or that issues need clarifying the leader should feel obligated to check with the "constituents" before moving ahead.

What has been said about the leader or the team manager applies to every group member as well. Since we are discussing professional teams operating as a community of equals and since each team member has collective and individual tasks to perform each person should feel free to proceed within his or her area of competence and freedom and to check with the group on those matters which require coordinating or which are of such significance that collective wisdom is necessary and desirable.

Within this framework let us look at some group methods which encourage individuals to involve themselves in solving problems or other group connected activity. Let us look first at a group methodology that has been called The Problem Solving Session.

The Problem Solving Session

The Problem Solving Session is a semi-structured meeting in which the leader provides the structural framework, but team members provide the substantive inputs. All members, leader and participants alike, assume responsibility for examining and dealing with the emotional tone of the meeting. Although not all problem solving sessions emerge in "mint" condition here are the steps generally followed.

Step 1—Setting the stage. Here we are talking about a leadership function that can be performed either by the designated leader or by several of the group members. The purpose is to develop an understanding of what the meeting is all about. This involves some notion of how the meeting was generated, for what cause and by whom. If there is a problem that has been predetermined by some authority this should be discussed. The group should know where it stands. If there are limits to the responsibility and authority of the group, members should know the nature of these limits. Insofar as possible group members should agree on the scope of their activities in terms of the problem. Hopefully the problem is one that has meaning for the group. After this "estimate of the situation" the group should be ready for the discussion question.

Step 2—Stating the question. The leader can help focus attention on the problems by writing the question to be discussed on newsprint or blackboard so that it will be before the eyes of the group and serve as a continuing point of reference. In writing the question a leader has the obligation to state it in a manner which is acceptable to the group. Preferably it is stated in problem rather than in threatening or accusing terms. For example, rather than writing "How can we get our project on schedule?" the question might be "What additional actions can we take to keep our project on schedule?" Although posing the question seems a simple thing it may be the key to successful or unsuccessful outcomes of the problem solving session. Here are some general considerations to keep in mind when developing the question:

1) The scope of the question should be limited to the:

    a. purpose of the group,

    b. capacity of group members and

    c. time available.

2) Misdirected effort, group frustration and uneconomical use of available time may result if the preceding three elements are not considered. At the same time the leader should frame the question in such a way that members will be able to explore all phases of the problem posed. The question should be phrased to:

    a. encourage discussion—in general an open-ended question stimulates more productive discussion than a question which can be answered by "yes" or "no." Posing the problem as a statement is not usually as effective as posing it as a question. The question implies action.

    b. avoid critical implications—the question should not imply a threat or criticism of or to the group.

    c. be positive—avoid negative wording such as "Why can't we?" Be positive. Approach the question as "How can we?"

d. make it personal—an abstract or impersonal question usually will stimulate less discussion than a question that personally and directly involves the participants.

e. keep it simple—a complex question or one involving vague words or qualifications tends to cause straying from the subject and provokes useless debate over definitions and meanings.

f. be brief.

3) Posing the question to the group is a symbolic act which leads the group into the next stage of discussion. Here the designated leader has a specific job to do:

a. write the question on the conference pad or blackboard,

b. repeat the question in the same words that appear in written form and

c. wait for the group to respond.

Step 3—Fact gathering. In problem solving it is very useful if the group disciplines itself to concentrate on gathering the facts before plunging toward a series of suggested solutions. With the question or problem to be engaged written on the newsprint, it is suggested that the group leader make a visible listing of the facts or opinions that are brought to light by group members. The group leader will neither censor nor "approve" contributions of individual members. In other words the leader does not make judgments concerning the significance or insignificance of the data proposed. The list that appears on the newsprint provides a summary of the circumstances involved in reaching a solution to the problem. The group is confronted with its own contributions and is in a position to judge whether such "facts" are relevant or irrelevant.

It is a good idea for the sheets to be torn from the conference pad as they are filled and placed in visible positions around the wall. This will keep them before the group during the session. The sheets will also be available for any additions group members wish to make as the session proceeds. It is always a good idea for the leader to number the items and to have one last number on the list which has not yet been written. This is a psychological invitation to group members to add other items as they occur.

If the problem is of some magnitude it might be worth developing a force-field analysis from the fact sheet. This would involve extracting from the list those items that were driving forces toward the solution of the problem and those forces which were restraining, working against the solution of the problem. When the group has exhausted its potential for contributing data it is time to think about action options or possible solutions to the problem.

Step 4—Action options. As soon as all the thoughts which the group believes to be pertinent are listed the leader can remind the group that it is time to undertake developing the field of options available for action. At this point the group is encouraged to state alternatives. These are also listed without censorship, but after they have been written on newsprint or blackboard it helps if the group member would state the reasons for making the proposal. This helps other participants understand the member's frame of reference. The group should not be asked to evaluate the suggested solution but rather to attempt to listen with understanding so that they see the proposals through the eyes of the proposers. At this state of the problem solving session each alternative suggested by a group member is recorded without giving it a value or putting it in priority form. The next step involves weighing the value of these contributions.

Step 5—Weighing the alternatives. The group leadership function in this step is largely procedural. There is a necessity to help the group focus on setting priorities. This probably should not be done until group members have an opportunity to "level" concerning their ideas and feelings on each possible approach. In extremely important matters it is even worthwhile to run another force-field analysis on each action option. The ideal, of course, is to talk the problem through to a true consensus rather than taking a vote. So after asking for expression of opinions concerning each proposed solution members should be asked to indicate their preference on first, second and third choices. By this process it is usually possible to narrow down the field and after a little more discussion of the three or four favorite solutions to again ask members to indicate their first priority. Almost always a distinct preference emerges in this process. If, however, there is an apparent difference that is significant to members of the group it is the responsibility of leadership to focus on differences and to try to discover an approach that will be mutually satisfactory to contending parties. Group leaders and group members should be working in an environment where the group "wins" rather than a contending environment in which some members win and some members lose.

There are occasions when one or two members, because of values or some other reasons, find it impossible to accept a solution proposed by the majority of group members. If consensus does not seem possible there are a couple of possibilities open to the group. One is to do nothing, which might mean that one or two people could "tyrannize" over the rest of the group. Or, more happily, it might be possible for both actions to be taken. In other words the majority group could do as it proposed. Obviously the nature of the problem and the circumstances of the group would indicate whether such a "split verdict" would be acceptable. In general it could be stated that consensus is desirable and should be the group goal. But failing consensus should not place the group in a doctrinaire position when some other decision making approach could also be satisfactorily utilized.

Step 6 — Action Step. The Action Step requires decisions on the part of the group as to what is to be done, how it is to be done, who will do it, when it will be done, where it will be done and what kind of feedback system will be developed to determine how well the task is being accomplished. Decision makers frequently make the mistake of not developing an understanding of precise target times for implementation and activities. A very vital part of each problem solving session involves the action step in which a schedule is laid out and an implementation methodology agreed upon.

General comments on use of the problem solving session. It will come as no surprise that the problem solving session is patterned on the "scientific method." One of the problems with the method is that it is very time consuming. It takes time to engage each step seriously. The method should not be undertaken unless this serious attempt is to be made. The effort involves obtaining the thinking of individual members and full deliberation by the group so that conclusions reached truly represent the general feelings of those present. Unless this occurs the problem solving conference becomes yet another game that people play. Effective use of the method requires considerable training of both group members and the designated leader.

Problem Census

Whenever an overview of opinions and problems is needed from a group the problem census provides an excellent means of bringing this about. The method serves to stimulate thinking and participation. It involves all group members and gives them an investment in the process. If the purpose is agenda development for the meeting it gives participants an opportunity to make sure their problems are considered. The method can be used in team building to catalog serious organizational and personal problems. As we have seen this particular method was incorporated into the problem solving session as part of the data collection process.

During the problem census the group leader should demonstrate a willingness and desire to hear and record the ideas of group members without evaluation or censure. The leader must show by his or her attitude and behavior that it is "safe" to contribute; by modeling a non-evaluative behavior the leader can assist in developing this attitude as a norm in the group.

This is how a problem census works:

Step 1. The group leader describes the process and cautions participants not to evaluate each other's contributions during the recording stage. Depending on the time available the group may wish to set a limit on the time to be spent in developing the list. After the leader opens the meeting to contributions he or she records all offerings (using conference paper or other means). The leader should try to abbreviate the items but at the same time catch the full sense of the ideas. There should be no show of impatience or criticism of ideas or of individuals.

Although it slows the process down to a certain degree it is generally a good idea to ask the person making the contribution to elaborate on its meaning. This must be done in a non-threatening way. The leader should first write down the person's statement; only after it is written down should the participant be asked to explain further. The items should be numbered. If the leader can stay one number ahead of the group the leader will encourage more contributions. The leader should check occasionally to see if any ideas were not recorded or if any contributions were improperly captured.

During the process suggestions may slow down. If the leader then asks, "Are all of the problems up here that we wish to consider?" frequently another flurry of items will result. When no more items are forthcoming the leader should leave a blank number at the end of the list and suggest that the group proceed to its next task.

Step 2. During the census, group members should check to be sure the items they suggested are recorded as they intended. Members should also avoid getting ahead of the recording. They can be helpful by careful and concise phrasing of statements and by waiting until one item is written before suggesting the next.

Step 3. When the list is complete the individual items may be briefly reviewed to clarify meaning. Illustrations may be given and similar items combined when the purpose is to set priorities on problems to be solved. A poll can be taken to see which of the problems seem to be most important to the greater number of participants.

Setting priorities is usually a difficult assignment for a group. One way is to ask each member to record the number of the two or three problems the member thinks most significant for discussion. As these selections are called off by the members the leader places checkmarks before the nominated items showing the number of persons declaring the item to be important. A ranking which serves as a priority usually results.

Step 4. After the priority is determined the group is ready to take up the discussion of the items.

Whoever is performing the recording function on the chart pad or newsprint becomes the focal figure in the group. It is fairly obvious that the communication flows between group members and the person who is doing the writing. When the list is completed and priorities are set the leader should move away from the chart, preferably across the room, and invite the members to take up the item that they considered most important. Then the leader should permit the interaction to grow between group members rather than be the center of the conversation.

During the recording of the participant ideas the chart papers, when filled, should be removed from the easel and taped around the room so that all ideas are visible at all times.

In some groups the contributions start slowly and this is the time for the leader to be patient and to "out wait" the group. Generally the problem is the reverse. Ideas come so fast that the recorder has difficulty in writing them down. If there is some reason for the designated leader to maintain the leadership in the group during the problem census this person should do the recording. Typically the person with the marker becomes the group leader.

Brainstorming

Brainstorming is a variation of the problem census but has a different purpose. Rather than delineating problems brainstorming is largely focused on creative and innovative solutions to problems. The idea of brainstorming was popularized in 1953 by Alex Osborne. Through the Creative Education Foundation Osborne applied brainstorming in a number of industrial and research organizations involving business, engineering, scientific and management problems (Osborne, 1953).[2] The popularity of the method has diminished, but under certain conditions it still has a place particularly when a team has reached the point at which stimulation and development of new and innovative ideas is a matter of organizational concern.

Here's how brainstorming works:

Step 1. The group leader writes the problem for which solutions are sought on the blackboard or chart paper. The question should be brief, specific and stimulating.

Step 2. The reason why the question is a matter of concern to the group or organization should be made clear to participants. Either the designated leader or other group members should provide all pertinent background information which participants might need and also explain how the ideas generated during the brainstorming session will be used.

Step 3. The ground rules for brainstorming should be clearly explained.

1) Every idea is acceptable (even if it sounds silly).

2) No evaluation of ideas is permitted by the group during the brainstorming period. This includes both verbal evaluation and non-verbal expression of approval or disapproval.

3) The quantity of ideas is the main goal—quality ideas will normally follow. This is called free-wheeling.

4) Building on the contributions of others is referred to as hitch-hiking and is encouraged. Some of the best suggestions result from the stimulation provided by the ideas of others.

5) Group members should be encouraged to think of "opposites" to ideas that have already been suggested.

6) A time limit for the brainstorming period should be set.

Step 4. The group leader lists each idea on the conference pad as quickly as possible. Contributions are written down exactly as given. Hesitation in recording the ideas sometimes gives the impression of disapproval. Usually the session begins with an initial spurt of ideas and then slows down. At this point a new flow of ideas may be stimulated if the group remains silent for several minutes and thinks about the problem and the ideas previously suggested.

Sometimes two recorders are used to speed the flow of ideas. In other groups tape recorders are used to capture the ideas. Although taping goes more rapidly it does not provide

100

the means of visual stimulation that comes from chart paper recording.

Step 5. The follow-through—Once ideas are expressed something must be done with them. The group can now evaluate the suggestions. As an alternative it can divide into sub-groups. Each sub-group selects ten of the most promising suggestions and reports results of its evaluation to the re-assembled group. It might then be possible for the group as a whole to arrive at a consensus. The method of evaluating and utilizing the ideas resulting from brainstorming depends, of course, upon the area of freedom of the group, the nature of the problem and the time available.

Brainstorming is applicable to task groups, staff meetings, problem solving meetings and meetings in organizations intended to explore possible courses of action. It is very useful for encouraging employee suggestions and for gaining participation by group members.

The Risk Technique (Maier, 1952)[3]

The risk approach to group meetings is so named because it involves a discussion of risks which surround a problem, policy or issue. In using the risk approach those involved address areas that are bothersome or anxiety generating. Although the name derives from the fact that risks are being explored there is yet another risk. This risk is that the people involved in the exercise may reject the organizational position, making it necessary to alter directions.

The risk approach is directed toward releasing expression of fears on the part of group members. It is very useful in discussing subjects where participants evince hostility or portray a general negative attitude. It is also useful as a way of getting possible objections to a program or proposal into the open, thus giving the group an opportunity to look at objectives and discuss feelings.

The approach is based on the assumption that the open expression of fears is not contrary to the acceptance of positive group goals. It is further assumed that repression of feelings, fears and resistance in a group represent a barrier to effective group action because individuals having such feelings are anxious or frustrated. Reaction to anxiety or frustration is often hostile, childish and stubborn rather than constructive and problem solving. The effect of producing a list of risks tends to clarify attitudes and reduce frustration. The principal objective of the risk technique is to develop a problem solving climate in the group as quickly and as effectively as possible.

This is how it works:

Step 1. A problem is presented to the group. This may be a supervisory problem in a work unit or it may be an organizational problem. Any time a new program procedure or process is being introduced to a working organization those involved in the introduction should consider the risk technique as a possible way of gaining understanding and commitment from those who will be affected by the innovation. For purposes of illustration let us say that the problem being presented to the group is one of whether to initiate an action research and training program in regard to the personnel system. In such a case the leader would ask a question like, "What are the dangers or risks involved in conducting an action training and research program in regard to our personnel system?"

Step 2. Each obstacle (or risk) is recorded on the chart paper, newsprint or blackboard as it is verbalized by the group participants. The leader is obliged to reflect the meaning and the intent of the person raising the risk question just as in the problem census.

1) After recording the essence of a risk the leader may ask the contributor to elaborate.

2) Some discussion may follow each risk item to determine the amount of support or the degree of feeling toward the statement by other members of the group. This discussion should involve statements of position but should not get into extensive argument over the merit of the item.

3) Every risk suggested should be recorded regardless of the group feeling about it. It is important that the discussion leader protect every individual's right to expression without fear of either the leader's or the group's censure.

4) As the chart paper or newsprint is filled it should be placed on the wall for the scrutiny of all who are present.

Step 3. Once all the fears are expressed and examined the newsprint should be removed from the wall with the leader assuring the group that if any other risk items occur to anyone these items will be recorded. This marks the end of the risk cycle. Presumably all of the doubts and fears that people have been able to conjure up during the session have been expressed and recorded. It should be apparent if the group is a low trust group that many risks will remain unspoken. On the other hand in a group in which good working relationships have been established the list will have considerable reliability.

Step 4. The group is now asked to examine the other side of the question. The leader proposes that since participants have looked at the dangers and obstacles to the Action Training and Research program in regard to the personnel system they should now develop a list of ideas as to how such a program might be undertaken in the face of those risks.

1) Again each suggestion is written on chart paper, newsprint or the blackboard and briefly discussed by the group as presented.

2) Upon completing the list the group may wish to arrange suggestions by priority, eliminate some suggestions as impractical or unnecessary, or choose one or two which they feel are of such merit as to demand immediate attention.

Step 5. The group members should decide what they wish to do about the problem, making specific plans to implement the decisions that they have made.

Sub-Grouping

Dividing a larger group into smaller sub-groups has utility under a number of circumstances:

1) Sub-groups can serve as an "ice breaker" method with people being able to get acquainted in groups of two or three. In such sub-groups there is more available "air time" per person, and many people feel a greater necessity to participate. Sometimes people who tend to be very quiet in a larger

group are able to express themselves in a sub-group.

2) Sub-groups are useful in dividing a large task into smaller bits, for example, having several work groups each developing a force-field analysis on one or more action options derived from a more lengthy list conceived by the larger group.

3) Sometimes hostile or critical views are more freely expressed in sub-groups where apparently a greater feeling of anonymity exists than in the group as a whole.

4) Sub-grouping sometimes serves to break the monotony of meetings, permitting people to move around and interact with other group members on a more intimate basis.

The size of the sub-group usually depends upon the size of the total community. In a large auditorium with movable chairs the sub-groups might number seven to ten people. In the same size auditorium with fixed chairs one appropriate division is to have three people talk together; one person in the middle can be talked around by those sitting on each side. In a large auditorium with the noise level being the factor it is the smaller the sub-groups the better the hearing for participants. If it doesn't get too complicated the groups probably should be smaller than ten, maybe five would be about the ideal. In a work group of say twelve people the sub-groups should be three per group.

There is no real evidence available on this. The group size is generally determined by rule of thumb. Robert Bales of Harvard has done some research on effectiveness of groups. His early findings were that groups of five to seven were the most effective. Long-term groups of three tend to make one of the members a scapegoat. This does not generally occur in sub-grouping since the people are not usually together long enough for group size to become a problem.

Sub-grouping then is another possibility to improve performance and group interaction. This is how it works:

Step 1. The large meeting is divided into sub-groups, assignments being made in a decisive way. Sometimes groups will indicate they do not wish to break into small groups. In this case the leader should accede to the will of the larger body.

There is a danger, however, that one or two members will object when the larger group would wish to participate in sub-grouping. This the leader must learn how to test so that tyranny does not exist.

Thus the group leader should think through in advance how to give instructions clearly for the sub-grouping. Groups may be formed by such simple devices as having people count off with all the number ones, number twos, threes, etc., congregating. Another way of forming groups is to designate locations for group meetings and ask people to sort themselves out in groups of the desired size.

Other very interesting ways which add to the fun of group life can be introduced. For example, all of the people who arrive at airports early can be asked to congregate on one side of the room, those who arrive late on the other. Generally the division of the house is about equal—but no matter. The next "cut" can be something like all those who are morning people, who get up early and work best in the morning, move to still another location, while those who are night people also move to another designated spot. Thus you have eight possibilities for groups and the two divisions. Then your own initiative and imagination on fixed types of categories can come into play, for example, all those who find themselves able to eat parsnips or all those who have blue eyes move to one direction, brown eyes to another, with hazel eyes remaining in place. These categories are illustrative and are simply given as an example of how to introduce a little humor into the sub-grouping process.

Step 2. Each sub-group is given a specific issue, problem or question. Several groups may be given the same question to discuss or each group may be given a separate issue.

Step 3. A time limit, depending on the time available and the difficulty of the subject-matter, is indicated to persons going into sub-groups. Information generated in sub-groups can be superficial if sufficient time is not given for the discussion. On the other hand if groups are allowed too much time they tend to divert themselves with inconsequential topics. This means that the group leader must be very alert to what is going on in the sub-groups. When they have exhausted a topic it is time to get the group as a whole into action.

Step 4. Each group is asked to nominate a reporter to present the results of the sub-group effort to the larger group. In reporting the small group discussion negative opinions expressed by individuals in the small groups may be given by the reporter without fear of revealing the identity of the individual holding that negative view. The reporter usually receives the support of the sub-group as long as he or she accurately summarizes its opinions and recommendations. Quite frequently a strong psychological unity will prevail among sub-group members. After the report general discussion, questions and evaluations are encouraged.

Sub-grouping is a very effective method for stimulating group interaction and group productivity. Those performing the leadership function should cherish this method but use it well. There are times when the total group needs to work as a unitary body, and in such circumstances splitting it into sub-groups is unfortunate. Leaders must strive to sense group needs and use sub-grouping accordingly.

Scenario Development

In some ways the development of scenarios becomes an individual rather than a group matter, and its usefulness as a group method depends upon the interaction that grows out of unilaterally developed scenarios.

A scenario as the term is used here is an individual's view of the future. A person imagines what the circumstances in an organization or project will be in a definite time horizon and writes this vision as a story. The person can be a principal actor or can put others in any role he or she wants. In a sense the scenario becomes the individual's "dream" of the future. Scenarios may be developed from a strict reality base or may be broad conjecture. What the scenario does is to bring aspirations into focus and permit dealing with personal agendas in a rather concrete way. For organizations attempting to institute a planning process the development of scenarios by significant actors can become a very substantial base for planning.

This is how the method works:

Step 1. The group is given an understanding of the nature of a scenario, the possible length and the due date.

Step 2. If possible all the scenarios written by group members are reproduced so that each person in the group has a copy. If not provision is made for each group member to read all the scenarios.

Step 3. Each group member presents his or her own scenario and receives comments for its improvement from the group as a whole.

Step 4. The group attempts to produce a composite scenario. One way of doing this is to note all of the events of every scenario on the horizontal dimension of a grid, with the names of persons on the vertical, with x's being noted where these overlap. Another way is to develop a census list in the development of priorities. There are obviously a number of methods of writing the composite scenario including the appointment of a sub-committee with group review. Some organizations have used the scenario approach in developing strategic plans from which operating plans are drawn.

The Case Method

The Case Method is an adaptation of a training approach which has been a mainstay in preparing persons for the practice of law. In the context of legal training the case approach involves a search of situations and court decisions which have a bearing on a particular type of case. The case highlights a set of circumstances and actions on the part of persons involved in the legal problems.

Christopher Langdell is credited as the innovator of the Case Method at the Harvard Law School in the 1880's. "This nondirective way of helping students to think for themselves slowly won acceptance in the study of Law, Medicine, Business Administration and Social Work." (Pigors, 1967).[4] Cases used in training take many forms. Some are long and are an effort to describe completely a situation that exists or did exist in the past. Other cases may be short and pungent of the vignette variety. In general the purpose of cases is the same. The participants read the materials, discuss the problems involved, consider the possible ramifications of a variety of decisions and finally are called upon to develop their own decision from which they are supposed to be able to generalize for future use. Sometimes the cases used by the leader are cases from outside the organization. Some cases, however, are written around the "immediate present" giving discussants an opportunity to delve into circumstances that apply to their own work situation.

Writing cases has become very complicated in the "Harvard" type cases. Investigators spend great amounts of time delving into organizational and historical settings in order to describe actions of the significant people involved, to uncover information concerning the origin of problems and to give a complete description of the organizational setting in which the action unfolded.

Obviously the more complicated the case, the more time that is likely to be consumed in the examination of circumstances involved and the arrival at a solution to the problems that are discovered.

The leader role in the case method is one of assisting students to look at the case, to feed back ideas and notions generated through discussion and occasionally to challenge students with questions concerning their observations. Since the setting is one in which the students are expected to develop the discussion they are more active than the group leader.

Sometimes the students are given a set of written questions to consider as they discuss the case material.

Step 1. All members of the group are given a case to read. This can be distributed in advance or time can be given at the beginning of the session for the group to read and digest the material. Along with the case material the leader can hand out questions which might help in the discussion of the case.

Step 2. Students are asked to discuss the case, with each student responding to the questions or giving his view of the circumstances and what he considers to be appropriate decision. The instructor and other group members challenge him on his views and require him to explain the reasons why he arrived at his decision. The group is asked to verbally generalize from the case and the discussions which followed.

Probably the case method is more useful in training situations than in task force work. Sometimes, however, a case can be used creatively in order to stimulate thinking which leads to future planning and project development. Such a case needs to be carefully drawn with the major problem and opportunity areas faced by the organization being thoroughly exposed and a frank portrayal of the parts played by various actors being written into the case.

The Incident Process

Faith and Paul Pigors developed a group method named *The Incident Process*. The method is flexible because incidents exist in every organization which may be used in the incident process.

The value gained from the use of the method may very well be greatest in the area of decision making, for it provides the participant with an orderly approach to problem solving. In addition to the practice of decision making the incident process helps develop knowledge and information concerning the problem under discussion. If the incident is a real one in the life of the organization the exercise provides a reality base that is often very helpful in a training session. As practiced by the Pigors the training group works as follows:

Step 1. The incident is passed out in written form. (Some trainers use a short role playing situation to introduce the incident.)

Step 2. Students are invited to make a short-term decision arrived at from the perspective of the person who, in the case, had to cope with the incident. This is usually the viewpoint of the main character who is involved.

Step 3. From the designated point of view the student begins to develop information by addressing questions to the session leader. The leader answers the questions but does not supply any information which is not requested. The leader has the needed facts because the leader either has prepared the incident or is familiar with a comprehensive case on which the incident was built.

Step 4. After the students believe they have developed all the necessary facts they are requested to formulate an issue around which the short-term decision will be made.

Step 5. Next students are asked to give their views of the nature of the problem. The students record their individual decision, and the decisions are shared. The leader attempts to sub-group the students into those who have made like-minded decisions. Together they develop information to support their decision.

Step 6. Generally there are several different points of view in any training group.

Step 7. Persons assuming different viewpoints are asked to debate.

Step 8. The designated group leader supplies the training group with information as to what "actually" happened in the original case or incident. No attempt is made to have the group develop a consensus or arrive at a group solution.

The incident approach is a leader-centered process. It is a useful way of stimulating interest in a particular situation. It is also an interesting, effective and unique way to give information to persons who, through the process, make themselves ready to receive the information.

Simulations

The group leader should be familiar with simulations since utilization of this process moves a step closer to "real life," permits participants to become emotionally involved and thus provides for learning at a significant level.

Some games or simulations are very sophisticated and expensive. They have been developed through extensive research and have been computerized so that participants may receive information concerning a developing situation, react to the information, feed this back to the computer and get "results" of the action to indicate the efficacy of the decision taken. The advantage of the sophisticated computerized games is that they can incorporate operation research techniques. In the not too distant future they will probably incorporate predictive models, which should help in gaining experience in decision processes.

Less sophisticated and less expensive are "In Basket" simulations. "In baskets" usually consist of a series of letters or documents that would normally appear in the in basket of the supervisor or manager. In the simulation exercise the participants are asked to act upon these documents as if they were actually in their own in baskets. If the in basket materials are carefully written to illustrate specific problems, they may be more valuable in changing behaviors and attitudes than comparable material derived from reading and discussing a traditional case would be. Preparation of in basket material however, should be as carefully done as is the preparation of any good and effective case material.

In general it may be said that "in basket" simulation should be fairly closely related to the kind of setting in which the group members participating in the exercise normally find themselves. This means that individually developed simulations are probably best and, of course, the most expensive. Other kinds of simulations use both prepared written material and role playing of simulated situations.

Role Playing

Role playing involves asking participants to assume the parts of other real or imaginary persons and to carry on conversations and behave "as if" they were these other individuals. Among the values to be derived by participants in role playing is the opportunity to learn by doing. In the process people develop data that influence their opinions about events. They are thus able to generalize the effect of their experience on both an intellectual and feeling basis.[5]

The ingenious trainer can develop roles which illustrate differences. For example, role players can be given the identical problems to solve but asked to do so with different kinds of leadership. Role playing of the interaction in response to each leadership style can be put on a tape recorder or on video tape and played back to note any differences or contrasts which develop from employment of different leadership modes.

111

"In basket" or simulation material often develops incidents that can be role played, and this enhances learning as well as interest in the simulation.

Role reversal is frequently used as a role playing device so that the principals can react to two different points of view. For example, the role playing could involve a government worker and a citizen. After participants have played these roles for a few minutes the roles could be reversed with the citizen become the government worker and the government worker the citizen.

Another approach to role playing is the replay which occurs after participants have had an opportunity to analyze behavior and the effectiveness of their first role played. Based on the learning that has taken place role players undertake the roles a second time and try to improve their initial performance.

Now that video tape has become more readily available it is often used in conjunction with role playing. Role players engage the role, and observe themselves as the action in which they were involved is reenacted before them. This "instant feedback" has tremendous impact on behavior and is particularly useful in creating a common group experience for discussing and diagnosing interpersonal problems. The feedback provides an opportunity to gain understanding and acceptance of the views of others. Role playing can provide a measure of preparation which can help people meet future problems, assume new roles and meet new situations. As in all role playing the enactment gives the participant practice in handling difficult situations, in becoming aware of problems and in trying out proposed solutions. A tape recorder is also very useful in playing back role enactments for analytical purposes.

Regardless of the role assigned the person always plays himself, at least partially. A principal in a role playing incident often recognizes this and sometimes some very useful insights develop.

It has been said that people have the natural desire to act. To the degree that this is so role playing dramatizes the situation that is being discussed or examined and has a tendency to involve and interest all persons in the training group whether or not they are actually playing the role. Those not engaged in the roles can analyze the points of view and the behavior of the role players. Role playing permits persons to experiment with how they would handle a given situation. In acting spontaneously role players often bring out feelings and attitudes which might not come out in regular discussions. For this reason role players and group members sometimes develop significant insights and even the ability to predict behavior patterns in themselves and others.

Persons who play roles frequently overact or characterize themselves. This is particularly true when hostile feelings exist. Hostility can be expressed in very subtle ways. When an employee takes the superior's role, the way the boss is caricatured often indicates hostile feelings that might exist about the superior. Sometimes role playing becomes a good diagnostic tool because it brings out the expression of latent feelings and attitudes. This seems to be the advantage derived from enacting rather than simply discussing a problem.

Sometimes individuals are reluctant to participate in a role playing exercise, but for the most part, after an initial period of anxiety, people begin enjoying the process. It must be noted, however, that there are individuals who seem to be unable to play roles and can only talk about what a person in that role would likely do. They truly find themselves unable to assume the role. When trainers encounter persons of this temperament they should not force these persons to participate.

Although there are many ways to introduce and conduct role playing from multiple to progressive roles, here in general is the way it is done:

Step 1. Verbally or in writing the leader describes the setting in which the action is to take place.

Step 2. Verbally or in writing the leader describe the persons who will be represented in the roles.

Step 3. The leader secures the people to play the various parts and makes sure that they understand the "point of view" or "part" which they will develop and play. Sometimes a conflict situation arises in a group and the two people involved in the conflict are then assigned to play each other's role. On other occasions people may be asked to volunteer for roles, or the group leader can in a good natured way volunteer for them.

Step 4. The persons who play the roles are asked to comment on the learnings and insights they gained during the role playing.

Step 5. Other participants in the group are asked to give feedback to the persons who played the roles.

The knowledge that a person obtains from participating in role playing is a personal knowledge. Therefore the participant must interpret the learning that took place.

Guided Discussion

Guided discussion is a leader-centered activity. The task of the leader in guided discussion is to ask questions and focus on issues in a manner that will lead to a specific learning or conclusion. Guided discussion is not suitable for decision making. It is a method used to cover material in a pedagogical manner so that the participant is required to think, respond and partially internalize the subject matter covered. Some of the best examples of guided discussion are to be found in a number of the Socratic dialogues. Guided discussion is most adeptly handled when the designated leader is thoroughly familiar with the subject matter and when he or she at least has a mental plan of questioning to reach the desired goal.

Here is how it works:

Leader: What is a guided discussion?

Student A: Guided discussion is a discussion directed by the teacher or leader.

Leader: What purpose is behind the direction thus provided?

Student B: To cover specific content areas in order to internalize such information or concepts.

Leader: Would you say that guided discussion is a modern instructional method?

Student C: It could be looked on as such.

Leader: What if I told you it was a very old method?

Student C: I would agree. Socrates used the guided discussion to teach his students in Ancient Greece.

Leader: Then why did you say it could be a modern method?

Student C: Because it is essentially the method that is used in the intrinsic approach to programmed instruction.

Leader: When should I use guided discussion as a decision making process?

Student A: Whenever you want the group to move quickly toward solution of a problem.

Student B: Your question confuses me.

Leader: You have a right to be confused. In my view the method is unsuitable for decision making. Can you speculate as to why I hold that position?

Student C: To me it would seem dishonest. You would be leading me toward a decision you already had in mind. I would not like to be manipulated in that manner.

Guided discussion is strongly leader-centered. Most of the interaction is between the leader and student on a one-to-one basis. The leader transacts with first one person then another. Only rarely do students in the group talk with each other. This means that the leader is in control of the group most of the time.

Free Discussion

In free discussion the members take the major responsibility for whatever action occurs in the group. In a mature group operating on a free discussion basis attitudes and values are expressed. With this type of interchange there is a clarification of existing forces at work in the group and the relationship between one person's values and those of others. In this setting the expression and exploration of hostile attitudes, fears and suspicions become a matter of obligation.

Free discussion can be used for gaining information; discovering or stimulating interest in or testing of ideas; reducing resistance, anxiety and fears; or developing group unity and consensus.

This is how it works:

Step 1. The group leader or other member convenes the group and introduces the topic. If the topic is simply discussion of anything a member wants to bring up this should be noted.

Step 2. The leader reduces his or her own psychological size. The leader's role is purely facilitative.

Step 3. The designated leader introduces and maintains a fully permissive climate.

Step 4. The leader models listening and leveling behavior.

Step 5. The designated leader focuses on process: reflects feelings of participants, focuses on conflicts and antagonisms, and clarifies developing items of conversation which will lead to understanding.

Free discussion places a heavier responsibility on the group member since the success or failure of the free discussion depends upon the cooperative effort of those present. Free discussion can also be utilized as a means of group development to move groups from the psychological mode of dependence toward interdependence. The leader should be aware of the processes involved in group development and expect a counter-dependent mode to take over in the group before it becomes fully functioning. Likewise the leader can expect that the group will regress to counter-dependency from time to time when experiencing a greater than usual degree of anxiety.

7. Options For Certain Group Situations

There is a growing "how to do it" literature which suggests to the group leader a whole series of games, exercises or learning devices which can be successfully used in groups. The more experienced leaders become the more it is possible for them to "invent" interventions which help a group in its goal accomplishment. Sometimes group leaders become so fascinated with their experimentation in group exercises that they fail to consider whether or not the exercise will help the group move where the group itself wishes to go.

Here two things are important. First, group leaders must be aware of the stage of group development and that they must have a theoretical basis for utilizing the type of intervention in a particular situation.

Secondly, leaders should have available in their "repertoires" a wide range of such games, exercises and devices which they can interject into the group life with meaning and skill at just the appropriate moment. In other words the agenda is not planned and structured with games, exercises and devices in mind; rather the leader is responsible for ascertaining the mood and the needs of the group and having available an appropriate activity for that occasion.

Another danger involved in discussing available options in a paper of this kind is the danger of limiting the leader's thinking to those items suggested or, perhaps worse, instilling the idea that responsibility for solving a group's dilemma is the responsibility of the designated leader. There are many times, perhaps more often than not, when the proper leader intervention is no intervention at all. There is a real possibility that the designated leader will introduce an activity simply because he or she wants to feel needed, not because the group needs him.

With that sort of caution in mind we will now somewhat reluctantly discuss some options that are available in certain group situations. There are situations which recur in group after group. The designated leader should be aware of such situations and be prepared with as wide a range of options as is possible. Some situations which recur again and again are the opening of the session, failing to deal with values, learning to give feedback, group tyranny, intra-group conflict, over- and under-verbal group members and counter-dependent behavior toward the group leader.

Pertaining to Values

We all tend to behave rather consistently in keeping with a set of rather firmly held internalized values. Within my school faculty, for example, it is possible to predict fairly accurately how faculty members will react to certain proposals simply because their values and philosophies suggest such a point of view. This means that in committee meetings arguments are frequently over minutia, when the real difference that exists is a difference in values between two opponents. It is rather useless to continue an argument over a detail when the difference stems from a lack of understanding or ability to deal with the values felt by another person. Although there will be some oscillation in a person's value profile it seems safe to say that generally a person who thinks traditionally and holds to traditional values will react to current problems from a traditional point of view and his or her behavior will be quite consistent. On the other hand a person who is rather *avant garde* in thinking and philosophy will also react to problems fairly consistently with such a value system.

It is very difficult to change a person's value system and probably in most groups an attempt to do so would turn out to be utterly futile, even if it seemed desirable (and probably this in itself would be very dysfunctional). What needs to be done then is to help people understand their value construct, to share this with others, and to deal with each other respect-

118

fully, based on the values we know each other hold. With this attitude it is easier to approach a problem. By searching we are able to see that while some possible solutions might be damaging to a value system other equally good solutions might not.

One option is simply to ask people to think about their values and discuss them with their fellow participants. This is usually very difficult for group members to do and sometimes is quite time-consuming, but under certain circumstances this may be the best way to approach the value question.

Another way is to construct your own "value inventory" putting together what I call a series of "outrageous propositions" made up of the most emotional issues that are current at the time. There is a danger of making a list of this kind even for illustrative purposes since history moves rapidly, but at this writing one would have questions on the energy crisis, abortion, free love, the new morality and "who's to blame" for inflation. These items are then listed on chart paper along with the following scale to which people are asked to respond:

1) Disagree absolutely.

2) Disagree somewhat.

3) Have no feeling or can't answer.

4) Agree somewhat.

5) Agree strongly.

Participants fill out the forms (frequently a blank piece of paper) which are passed to the leader who shuffles and redistributes them in such a way that it is not likely that any group member gets his or her own paper. A count is then taken of answers by asking people to raise their hands to note the answer to each item on the paper they hold. Members are then asked to form into sub-groups to discuss the total value stance of the group as revealed by the tally and to speculate concerning the point of view evidenced by the person's answers on the individual sheet the participant is holding. What type of person is the participant? Flexible? Inflexible? Liberal? Conservative? Consistent? Another option is to place group members in triads or diads and ask them to interview each other on felt values and to report these back to the larger group.

119

When the group re-assembles members report on the nature and substance of the discussion in the small group. If it appears there is a climate which is sufficiently attuned, participants are asked to guess who is the author of the paper they are holding among the other group members and why they think so. This allows stereotypes to come out in the open. It also allows people to remain anonymous if they wish, or to freely admit, "Yes, that's my form and this is what I believe." Generally the process surfaces many of the more emotional values. As a result of the exercise group members have been able to learn a great deal about their own values and the values of others, and they tend to keep these in mind as the discussion proceeds.

Feedback

One of the major responsibilities of the designated leader is to help the group develop a feedback or internal righting system. The leader does this by helping a group learn the nature of feedback, and by modeling behavior. If the feedback is inadequate then the group will lose the benefit of an opportunity to improve its functioning. If the feedback is ineptly done it may be harmful, for it is not a psychoanalytic exercise. There is no place for interpretation of another's behavior. _No one can know another person's intentions_. In any transaction where intentions are attributed to a person, the attribution is first likely to be wrong and secondly to intrude upon the development of a working relationship.

Feedback should consist of what can be observed and what one feels. I can tell you what I see and what I hear. I can also reliably tell you what I feel about it. Those are bits of data that are useful.

Here are some options for the leader in developing the group's capacity for giving and utilizing feedback.

1) The designated leader can demonstrate how to give feedback by actually giving it. In other words, he can model the behavior. Sometimes in a very early intervention in this regard it is useful to discuss the concept of feedback, particularly as the process has been described by George Lehner (Lehner, 1974).[33]

120

2) There is a highly desirable option of using projection devices. One such device is asking group members to draw a self-portrait, posting these portraits around the room and asking other members to tell whose portrait each one is and why they think so.

3) Group members are sometimes asked to keep diaries, spending a few minutes at the end of each day or major session to write their feelings and impressions. These diaries are shared with the group.

4) Several kinds of charts are used to "draw a picture" of what is occurring in the group. For example, it is possible to chart the type of role taken by various group members such as clarifier, defender, initiator, gate-keeper, punisher or blocker.

Another kind of charting shows who is talking to whom and how often. Sometimes this indicates a very heavily leader-centered interaction with tall lines going to and from the leader. Sometimes it shows one or more persons are dominating the conversation while others have said nothing.

5) It is often very useful to stop and take a poll or reading of how people perceive the group functioning. One way of doing this is to construct a scale from one to five with one being low and five being high and to ask people to place their level of satisfaction at some point on the scale. If the cluster of answers is at the low end it gives the group an opportunity to take corrective action. If the answers are at the high end the group might wish to proceed with its present activities. These scales can be made for almost any type of activity. For example, they may be used to determine what the group's level of expectation is for any given session.

Tyranny

The word tyranny sounds sinister but tyranny in the group is not always a contrived and sinister activity. Usually the tryanny stems from the activities of cliques or of people who have a strong agenda in one direction or another. Those involved are likely to be very verbal people who consistently try to move the group in a direction which seems to them to be desirable. On some occasions it may be quite clear that the majority of the group wishes to go in one direction, say to break up into small groups, while the tyrannizers do not. Tyrannizers then block group action by objecting and prolonging discussion, raising questions and creating issues. In dealing with group tryanny here are some options available to the group leader:

1) Although the option of doing nothing is always available, in every predictable and recurring situation it is particularly well to keep this option in mind when tyrannizing raises its ugly head. Frequently a group has a way of struggling, becoming frustrated and finally resolving the tyrannizing without the help of the leader.

2) On those occasions when it appears the group does not know how to resolve the tyranny issue the designated leader may try to expel pluralistic ignorance by helping each member of the group express himself on the issue. By doing so it then might become clear that 90 percent of the group members favor a position quite opposite to that of the tyranny group. The leader needs to demonstrate in this instance that he or she cannot be tyrannized since it is likely that one or more members of the tyranny sub-group will try to keep the leader from taking a reading of group opinion.

3) This might be a good time to try a level of satisfaction chart.

4) "Going all different directions together" is a frequent state in a learning community where there is a wide variety of activity preferences. There is almost always a drive to compel the group to some standardization. There are, of course, times when the total group should be engaged in the same activity, but there are also times when it might be better for it to do a variety of things. Generally in group work one of the major efforts is to work from a consensual base. However, if it becomes clear that the group is polarized then a viable option is to let people have an opportunity to agree to disagree and to learn that sometimes it is all right to do the same thing in a different way (or for that matter different things in different ways).

Conflict

The designated leader's role in a conflict situation is to help people learn to utilize conflict constructively. There are several options that the leader should not undertake. One is either to ignore or permit the group to develop a norm of ignoring conflict situations. The leader should not be a party to the suppression of conflict. Nor should a leader try to get people to feel they understand each other or that they are "saying the same thing" when in fact they are miles apart.

It is important that the designated leader or others in the group recognize when a conflict situation exists and make every effort to deal with it directly. One way to do this is to point up the differences that exist between contending parties. Another is to recognize the feelings that are generated by the conflict. Here are illustrations of options available in dealing with conflict:

1) The leader might feed back to each party in the conflict what he or she has heard them saying and what appear to be their points of view. Through this process the leader can help the opponents express themselves, fully demonstrating what can occur when persons are willing and able to listen to what is being said by the persons with whom they are in conflict.

2) A role playing situation can be developed in which there is a role reversal with each person asked to take the role of the other. A variation of this, but probably not as meaningful, is to have two third-party observers take the role of the conflict principals so that the parties in conflict realize how they are being seen by others in the group.

3) The leader might utilize "Roger's rule" wherein opponents are asked to state to the satisfaction of the other person what that person's point of view appears to be on the matter under contest. This usually takes a little working through and is not easily accomplished, but when the task is done there is generally a much better understanding of the two points of view.

4) The leader might assist the contestants in sorting out the values that are being impinged upon or which are influencing the positions being taken.

Over-Verbal and Under-Verbal Behavior

People vary a great deal in their propensity to communicate in groups. In almost every group there is a range from the active verbal to the inactive verbal types. No law requires a person to participate any given amount, but the quality of group action depends a great deal upon the contribution of each member. Some people have the ability and apparently the need to speak out in large gatherings, others operate best in groups of 10 to 15, while still others are almost silent unless they are in an intimate group of two or three people. There are those who are such compulsive talkers that they completely dominate a group leaving little "air time" for the larger number of members.

The better functioning groups are those where a range of active participation exists, but in which no one is completely silent and no two or three people dominate the conversation. When confronted with an over-verbal member the group might do the following:

1) Keep a participation chart and show the degree of participation by each member or

2) Give direct feedback to the person as to how members feel about the domination.

3) The designated leader could help the over-verbal person retire to the background by stepping in and giving assistance to others who appear to wish to talk. This can sometimes be done by "bridging" or showing the connection between what several members of the group are saying, focusing attention on issues in which the group generally appears to be interested.

4) Try to deal with the over-verbal person by direct feedback from the group but not repeatedly confronting over-verbal behavior. Some group leaders have found to their sorrow that by trying to focus repeatedly on such behavior, more of this person's needs are met. In such groups this person not only dominates but also is the focus of continuing feedback (which he or she rejects, and the process turns out to be a group disaster.

Options for the under-verbal member include the following:

124

1) The designated leader and others in the group who are sensitive to the situation should be constantly aware of nonverbal signs given by the under-verbal member. When it appears as if that person has something to say the leader can say, "It looks as if Elizabeth was about to say something," thus providing a shield for Elizabeth to get into the conversation if the leader's reading was accurate.

2) Whenever an under-verbal person makes a comment (which is often ignored and glossed over by someone else in the group) the designated leader can feed back what the under-verbal person has said showing that the statement has been understood. This is also a good time to do some bridging between the statement made by the under-verbal person and contributions that have been made by others in the group.

3) The "air time" chart is frequently a vehicle which stimulates a conversation about the level of participation and gives the under-verbal person a safe opportunity to discuss the reason for his or her reticence. This alerts the entire group to the situation and group members begin to be sensitive to the under-verbal person's need to participate.

Counter-Dependent Behavior in Relation to the Leader

If the group is functioning well the designated leader should be prepared for any counter-dependent behavior which group members aim at him or her. There are probably a number of options open, but one of the most useful is to demonstrate that group members may in fact attack the designated leader. By his or her behavior the leader shows first that he or she hears what members are saying and second that it is their right to say it. As the group matures the leader might also wish to convey some of his or her own feelings, but this should not be done in a punitive way. If the leader appears to be highly defensive his or her behavior will probably interfere with group functioning.

8. Audio-Visual Devices

Judicious use of audio-visual methods can improve group productivity and increase learning, *provided*.... The "provided" is most important, for just as there is a temptation to utilize games, exercises and other structured activities as ends in themselves the same temptations occur when audio-visuals are used. In this wonderful electronic age there are innumerable types of audio-visual equipment available. Among the most useful audio and visual devices for the group leader are newsprint and chart paper, chalk-boards, tape recorders, video tape recorders and overhead projectors.

Newsprint and chart paper. Newsprint and chart paper are almost indispensable items for efficient functioning of groups. The best arrangement is an easel with a pad of paper attached. The paper should be scored so that it is easily removed from the chart pad. The easel should be light so it can be readily moved to any part of the room. *El Marco*

Felt tip pens or crayons should be available, preferably in two or three colors. If felt tip pens are used they should be of the type which do not "bleed" through the paper.

The training room should also be equipped with a roll of masking tape. Prior to any session in which newsprint may be used the masking tape should be torn into two-inch segments and placed along side the easel along the wall where newsprint might be hung. This is done in advance because it becomes rather awkward to remove the tape from the roll as the newsprint is being hung.

There are a few simple but important things to keep in mind in using the chart pad:

1) When writing on the paper stand to one side of the chart so that persons in the group can see what you are writing.

2) If you are talking when you are writing be sure that you are looking at the group rather than at the chart board. When you face the chart board it is often difficult to hear what you are saying. These actions are obviously more difficult for left-handers to follow but they should do their best.

3) Before using the chart paper carefully start to tear the top sheets which will be used along the perforations at the top of the pad. This should be done an inch or two from each side. When tearing a sheet from the pad PULL DOWN from the righthand side as you grasp the paper at the bottom of the sheet at approximately the middle. The tension toward the righthand side will cause the sheet to tear straight across so that the writing at the top of the page will not be mutilated and it will be easier to tape a straightly torn sheet to the wall.

4) Attach the masking tape to each top corner before placing it on the wall; then affix the tape to the wall by pushing upward with each thumb as you hold the paper on both sides and are facing the wall.

5) Write large enough on newsprint so that anyone in any part of the room can read what you are writing.

6) If you use a felt tip pen make certain that you re-cap it when you finish writing. This keeps the felt from drying out.

It is well to remember that the chart pad can become the symbol of the leader. If the designated leader of the group always sits by the chart pad this becomes the head of the room. It is far better if the designated leader moves around the room or that the chart pad be placed just outside the circle in a way that makes it the property of all group members. Under particularly affluent conditions it is even a good idea to have more than one easel.

For short presentations it is sometimes a good idea to make flip charts in advance on the chart paper. These can serve as notes as well as giving emphasis to the remarks that are being made. The charts can also serve as points of reference during the discussions which follow. When using tables, schemas or other illustrations to emphasize or clarify points keep them simple. It is very easy to clutter a page of newsprint and thus negate the advantages of graphic illustration.

Another way of using newsprint in connection with a presentation, is to make your charts as you talk. This is extremely effective because the group generally follows what you are doing verbally as well as visually. The act of writing itself attracts attention. Sometimes it is useful to write lightly penciled notes on the chart pad to remind yourself of points that should be made.

All eyes are likely to be focused upon the leader standing by the chart pad. Group interaction will thus be between the leader and individuals within the group. When it is time for the group to deal with the subject matter and to interact with each other then by all means the leader must sit down. It is even better if the leader moves away from the proximity of the chart pad.

Chalk board. A chalk board can be utilized much as the chart board, the major disadvantage being that the material cannot be kept for future reference. The chalk board should be used to record transient thoughts which supplement what is written upon the chart pad, or it should be used for material which can be contained on the space available and used for one session of the group.

Chalk boards are even more tyrannical than chart pads and easels because they are not portable. Most of us are conditioned to look on the chalk board as being the head of the room, just as it is in the normal classroom.

Tape recorders. As audio-visual devices go, the new compact casette recorders are very reasonable in price as are the tapes, which are conveniently carried, used and stored. The normally functioning recorder will pick up the conversation in a small group meeting. It can be used either to record the events of the meeting or as an instrument for play back. Those recorders which have counters are best for feedback purposes. A person observing the group can designate a place of interest by writing down the number appearing on the counter; thus the whole tape does not have to be re-played but only those spots which are of particular interest for feedback purposes.

It is surprising how soon groups become accustomed to having their conversations taped. Even so there are ethical questions involved. The material that appears on the tape is the property of the group unless an agreement has been made to use it for other purposes. The group leader is professionally bound not to allow others to hear the tape nor to transcribe portions of it without the full knowledge of those who have participated in the session.

The cassette recorder is particularly useful as a device in helping people "learn to listen" and to "level."

There are commercially prepared materials appearing in cassette form. These have all of the disadvantages of lectures without the advantage of personal appearance. They do have the unique feature of being available whenever a person would like to use them. In preparing material for this type of use it is probably well to build in some type of involvement for the listener and to keep the "telling" process short. A 15-minute attention span is probably very long for this type of presentation unless some type of involvement for the listener is built into the exercise.

In utilizing recorders one should keep in mind:

1) Check the functioning of all recorders to be used well in advance of the session.

2) Ascertain if electrical outlets are present, or if the recorders are battery powered, to be sure that the batteries are alive.

3) When several recorders are used in one room the groups using them should be sufficiently separated that a minimal amount of noise will be picked up from other groups.

4) In a playback to a total group the quality can be enhanced if the tape is played back through a public address system. This will even enable one to play back material in a large auditorium.

5) The recording heads on most recorders need cleaning periodically. The method of cleaning varies from model to model, and the manual or your dealer should be consulted on how to effect the cleaning.

Video-tape. Video-tape is a very dramatic means of providing feedback on group participation and interaction. The medium can be used to record interviews, role playing, presentations, or group interaction.

Participants tend to be a bit more conscious of the camera than they are of an audio-tape recorder, but after a while the group seems to become sufficiently accustomed to the camera to act naturally.

One of the major advantages of the video-tape is its ability to pick up non-verbal as well as verbal interaction. Through its use it is possible to illustrate to a group many of the factors involved in group dynamics.

There are packaged video-tape programs which have some utility but it is also possible to tailor some "lecturettes" to a particular group's usage. These lecturettes might even grow out of group's history or group interaction. When played back to the group these can be stopped and discussed as the group desires.

When video-tape is used extensively in a group, it is a very useful practice to have group members learn to use the camera. This gives the participant special practice in observing non-verbal behaviors and also seems to lessen the threat that might attend the recording of the session.

The ethics for the use of video-tape are the same as for using other recording means.

Overhead projectors. Overhead projectors are especially valuable to pick up typed or mimeographed material and project it for viewing and use by the entire group. Transparencies can even be made in color, and they can be made from the printed page by almost any copying machine. Overhead projectors have the advantage of allowing a person to face a group and still project the material.

There are a couple of cautions to keep in mind in regard to

the use of the overhead projector. First the print for the transparency should be large enough to be seen by the group. Although typing in the normal type face will project it usually is too small to be readily seen in a conference room. Therefore material for transparencies should be typed in one of the very large type faces available on some typewriters. Another problem with overhead projection use is the tendency to revert to one-way communication. The focus of the group is obviously on the projected material and toward the presenter. It is better to structure any presentation so that the group can engage in active discussion of the projected material rather than having it presented to them. Also, some people are bored by overhead presentations since they have been exposed beyond "endurance" to them in the military or in other organizational contexts.

General comments. Audio-visual materials that are generated in the group are far more effective from a learning and development standpoint than materials which are prepared for, and presented to, a group. Frequently, audio-visual materials are too "slick" and are thus seen as part of a sales or promotion job.

Although these paragraphs are salted with statements of great caution, the leader should still be encouraged to learn to use and work with audio-visual materials. Their appropriate and proper use can greatly enhance learning and aid decision making. Without the use of audio-visual technology the group will be deprived of a major resource.

Straight Talk About Logistics

Every designated leader should know that in conference work it is the "little things" that will kill you. Rooms that are not properly arranged or are not ready for occupancy, registration processes that are unwieldy, lack of ashtrays, coffee not available when expected, equipment that doesn't work, bad meals, poor living arrangements or inadequate pre-session communications are all factors that loom large in determining the success or failure of the meeting. They are so important that these details should be checked with vigilance. While it may not make sense to have the vice president in charge of industrial relations or the city manager personally check on these matters, he or she should at least be sure that someone does. Taking care of these minor but extremely important details is not overly time-consuming. Group leaders should develop a check list of items to be arranged and of equipment to be available for sessions.

Very good meetings have literally been ruined because of poor physical arrangements or and because conference planners did not check out the quality of food. A beautiful setting, comfortable accommodations and excellent food will not necessarily make a good program, but they certainly will help.

After the group or work team is formed it can help assume the logistical and housekeeping duties, and it is better if they do so. But in the beginning the burden is on the convenor.

DON'T SAY WE DIDN'T WARN YOU!

References

1. Values and Motivation

1. Eric Fromm, *Escape from Freedom* (London: Rutledge and Kegan, Paul, 1950).

✓2. Harry Stack Sullivan, *The Interpersonal Theory of Psychiatry* (New York: W. W. Norton & Co., Inc., 1953, pp. 208-211).

3. Abraham H. Maslow, *Motivation and Personality* (New York: Harper and Row, 1954).

4. Douglas McGregor, *The Human Side of Enterprise* (New York: McGraw-Hill, 1960).

5. Kurt Lewin, *Field Theory in Social Sciences* (New York: Harper and Row, 1948).

6. Rodney W. Napier and Matti K. Gershenfield, *Groups: Theory and Experience* (Boston: Houghton Mifflin Co., 1973, p. 226).

7. R. A. Johnson, F. E. Kast and J. E. Rosenzweig, *The Theory and Management of Systems* (New York: McGraw-Hill Book Co., 1963, pp. 4-6).

8. Magoroh Maruyama, "The Second Cybernetics: Deviation Amplifying Mutual Causal Processes," in *American Scientist,* 51 (1963), pp. 164-79.

9. Daniel Katz and Robert L. Kahn, *The Social Psychology of Organizations* (New York: John Wiley & Sons, Inc., 1966, p. 184).

10. B. F. Skinner, *Beyond Freedom and Dignity* (New York: Alfred A. Knopf, 1971, pp. 62-63).

11. Ernest R. Hilgard, *Theories of Learning* (New York: Appleton Century Cross, 1956, pp. 276-77).

12. Morton Deutsch and Robert Kraus, *Theories in Social Psychology* (New York: Basic Books, Inc., 1956, pp. 52-53).

13. Ibid., pp. 78-124.

14. Ibid., pp. 78-124.

2. Leadership and Membership

1. Herbert A. Thelen, *Dynamics of Groups at Work* (Chicago: University of Chicago Press, 1954, p. 296).

2. Daniel Katz and Robert L. Kahn, *The Social Psychology of Organizations* (New York: John Wiley and Sons, Inc., 1966, p. 302).

3. Herbert A. Thelen, *Dynamics of Groups at Work* (Chicago: University of Chicago Press, 1954, p. 297).

4. Jack R. Gibb, "Dynamics of Leadership," in William B. Eddy, W. Werner Burke, Vladimir A. Dupre and Oren South (eds), *Behavioral Science and the Manager's Role* (Washington, D.C.: NTL Institute for Applied Behavioral Science, 1971, p. 131).

5. Elizabeth Mann Borgese, "The Promise of Self-Management," in *Center Magazine*, May/June 1972.

3. Dynamics of Groups at Work

1. W. R. Bion, *Experiences in Groups* (New York: Basic Books, 1961).

2. Warren Bennis and Herbert Shepard, "A Theory of Group Development," in *Human Relations*, Vol. IX, No. 4, November 1956, pp. 421-23.

3. Ibid., pp. 421-23.

4. Leon Festinger and Elliot Aronson, "The Arousal and Reduction of Dissonance in Social Contacts," in Dorwin Cartwright and Alvin Zander (eds), *Group Dynamics Research and Theory* (Evanston, Illinois: Rowe, Peterson and Co., 1960, p. 216).

4. Communication in Groups

1. Daniel Katz and Robert L. Kahn, *The Social Psychology of Organization* (New York: John Wiley and Sons, Inc., 1966, p. 228); quoting Walter Lippman in *Public Opinion* (New York: Harcourt Brace, 1922, pp. 31, 90, 104-5).

2. Abraham Kaplan, NTDS Lecture, Snowmass, Colorado, August 1972.

3. Daniel Katz and Robert L. Kahn, op. cit., p. 223.

4. Herbert A. Thelen, *Dynamics of Groups at Work* (Chicago: University of Chicago Press, 1954, p. 319).

5. George Lehner, "Aids for Giving and Receiving Feedback," in Fred Fisher and Roy Gregg, *Managing Change* (Washington, D.C.: NTDS Press, 1974).

5. Methodology

1. Donald Nylan, J. Robert Mitchel and Anthony Stout, *Handbook of Staff Development and Human Relations Training Corps Materials Developed for Use in Africa* (Washington, D.C.: NTL Labs, pp. 269-70).

2. Robert Tannenbaum, Irving R. Weschler and Fred Massarik, "The Role of Trainer," in Golembiewski and Blumberg (eds.), *Sensitivity Training and Laboratory Approach* (Itaska, Ill., F. E. Peacock, Inc., 1970).

3. George F. Lehner, op. cit.

4. Neely Gardner, *Implementation: The Process of Change* (paper presented at Conference on Court Studies, Denver, Colorado, 1973, p. 12).

5. Ibid., pp. 17-18.

6. Warren Bennis, *Organizational Development: Its Nature, Origin and Prospects* (Reading, Massachusetts: Addison-Wesley Publishing Co., 1960, p. 2).

7. Gardner, op. cit., p. 19.

8. Ibid., p. 19.

9. Robert R. Blake and Jane Srygley Mouton, "A Behavioral Science Design for the Development of Society," in *Journal of Applied Behavioral Science*, 7:2, 1971, pp. 146-63.

10. Fred E. Emery and E. L. Trist, "The Causal Texture of Organizational Environments," in *Human Relations*, Vol. 18, 1965, pp. 21-32.

11. F. E. Emery and Eric Trist, "The Environment of the System," in (F. E. Emery, ed.) *Systems Thinking*. (Har-

mandworth, England: Penguin Books, Ltd., 1970, p. 256).

12. Gardner, op. cit. pp. 22-23.

13. Peter Drucker, *The Practice of Management* (New York: Harper and Row, Publishers, 1954, pp. 121-136).

14. Neely Gardner, *Management by Results* (paper delivered at the Federal Executive Institute, June 1972).

15. Douglas McGregor, *The Human Side of Enterprise.* (New York: McGraw-Hill Book Company, 1960, p. 46).

16. Neely Gardner, *Implementation: The Process of Change* (paper presented at "Conference on Court Studies" May, 1973. pp. 20-22).

17. Eric Berne, *The Games People Play.* (New York: Grove Press, 1964, p. 29).

18. Thomas A. Harris, *I'm O.K. – You're O.K.* (New York: Harper and Row, Publishers, 1967, p. 15).

19. Ibid, pp. 20-21.

20. Eric Berne, *Transactional Analysis in Psycho-therapy* (New York: Grove Press, 1961).

21. Harris, op. cit., p. 31.

22. Ibid., p. 36.

23. Berne, op. cit., p. 24.

24. Abraham Levitsky and James Simkin, "Gestalt Therapy," in Lawrence N. Soloman and Betty Berzon (eds.) *New Perspectives in Encounter Groups* (San Francisco: Jossey-Bass, Inc., Publishers, 1972, p. 15).

25. A. Levitsky and Fritz F. Perls, "The Rules of the Game in Gestalt Therapy," in J. Fagan and I. L. Shepherd (eds.), *Gestalt Therapy Now* (Palo Alto, California: Science and Behavior, 1970, p. 140).

26. Levitsky and Simkin, op. cit., p. 246.

27. Robert S. Blake and Jane Srygley Mouton, *The Managerial Grid* (Houston, Texas: Gulf Publishing Co., 1964).

28. Ibid., pp. 8-9.

6. Group Leadership Methods

1. Much of the material contained in the section on leadership methods was adapted from an earlier manuscript of the author entitled, "Management of Change" (Los Angeles: University of Southern California, 1969).

2. Alex Osborne, *Applied Imagination* (New York: Creative Education Foundation, 1953).

3. The risk approach was conceptualized by Norman R. F. Maier and is explained in some detail in his book, *Principles of Human Relations* (New York: Wiley and Sons, Inc., 1952, pp. 62-82).

4. Paul Pigors, "The Case Method," in Robert L. Craig and Lester R. Bittel (eds.), *Training and Development Handbook* (New York: McGraw-Hill Book Co., 1967, p. 174).

5. Lehner, op. cit.

9. Background Resources for the Group Leader

There are a number of books and articles of which the group leader should be aware. Some of these publications have to do with theory, others with "how to do it" exercises and games. Group leaders who are able to function best in participative situations are those who 1) understand group theory and 2) have knowledge and skill in introducing and using a rich variety of exercises, processes and games at appropriate times during the group's life. The following list is not exhaustive. One can be certain that new publications will continue to be developed, and these too will add to the leader's store of useful knowledge.

- Chris Argyris, *Integrating the Individual and the Organization* (New York: John Wiley and Sons, Inc., 1964).

Since the time when he conducted the research which culminated in the writing of *Personality and Organization* Chris Argyris has been doing studies and speculating about how organizations might be redesigned to take into account the energies and competencies individuals have to contribute. His tentative thinking is outlined in *Integrating the Individual and the Organization*. Since concepts of facilitative group leadership and organizational democracy are so closely related this book becomes important because it addresses many of the factors which lead to employee alienation. The Argyris "Mix Model," which is a conceptual organizational scheme, is an interesting start down the road to finding a pattern for organizations of the future.

The table of contents will help the reader visualize the scope of the Arygris book.

Table of Contents

Part One:
1. Introduction to Individual and Organizational Effectiveness
2. The Input
3. The Organizational Dilemma

This book also has a name and subject index.

• Richard Beckhard, *Organizational Development* (Reading, Massachusetts: Addison-Wesley Publishing Company, 1969).

Organizational Development is one of six volumes published as a group in the so-called Addison-Wesley Series on Organization Development. Beckhard is one of the best-known consultants in the O.D. field and in this book has done a straightforward and pragmatic job of setting forth his own point of view. Naturally Beckhard's view of O.D. is a reflection of his own practice, which has been singularly effective. The group leader should find the section "Organization Development Strategies at Work" particularly helpful, both conceptually and practically.

Table of Contents

● Warren G. Bennis, Kenneth D. Benne, Robert Chin, eds. *The Planning of Change*, 2nd edition (New York: Holt, Rinehart and Winston, Inc., 1968).

This is a collection of readings which points to the merging and reconciling of the arts of social practice and the sciences of human behavior. Essays, therefore, present discussions of change technologies in their intellectual, practical and moral bearing situation. Also, the editors have attempted to present articles which help persons learn more about functioning as change agents. Forty-three amazingly relevant articles form the substance of this publication. While many of the articles included in this volume may be found elsewhere the book holds together as a remarkably good reference for those who need to know more about the processes of organizational change.

143

Table of Contents

144

• Warren G. Bennis, *Organization Development: Its Nature, Origin and Prospects* (Reading, Massachusetts: Addison-Wesley Publishing Co., 1969).

Bennis calls this book a primer of Organization Development. A primer it may be, but it is a primer that does an excellent job of setting forth what O.D. purports to be about. As all books in the Addison-Wesley series the Bennis book is short (82 pages) and quickly read.

Table of Contents

• Robert R. Blake and Jane Srygley Mouton, *The Managerial Grid* (Houston, Texas: Gulf Publishing Company, 1964).

A few years back it might have been difficult to convince some trainers and managers that the grid approach to organization development represented one of several useful methodologies rather than the "Holy Writ." The strength as well as the weakness of the grid resides in its oversimplification. Managers understand the concept of the 9/9 administrator as the person who has high concern for people and for production. The Blake and Mouton instrumented approach to training generally is highly acceptable to administrators and often opens the door of an organization to the use of other developmental methodology. The danger, or at least annoyance, stems from the penchant of participants to label their colleagues as 1/9, 9/1 or even 1/1 (1/9 represents a minimal concern for production and a high concern for people; 1/1 is concern for neither).

The book deals with the grid as an instrument for orienting managerial actions by comparing major alternatives available for achieving production through people. It also shows how the grid may be used by readers to measure their own managerial style and how through educational effort an organization can achieve organizational excellence. The book appears to be a

146

training guide, a declaration of faith, a statement of theory and a low-key sales pitch.

Table of Contents

This book has an authors' index and a subject index.

• Robert R. Blake and Jane S. Mouton, *Group Dynamics—Key to Decision Making* (Houston, Texas: Gulf Publishing Company, 1961).

The team of Blake and Mouton authored this 112-page book around the notion that better decisions are a function of participation and communication. They suggest that a group dynamics laboratory is a means of training managers to communicate and participate. The laboratory is a replica of the human side of an organization which provides a means of acquiring knowledge as well as an opportunity for obtaining feedback on one's own behavior. One interesting feature of the book is the degree to which it emphasizes the power aspect of the organization. Blake and Mouton provide examples of questionnaires that may be used in a group to stimulate the feedback process. They also show how the data generated by the questionnaire can be looked at by participants.

This book is easily and quickly read and might be one which the boss could read, too, for orientation concerning some of the possibilities of team effort.

Table of Contents

This book has a glossary of terms and a subject index.

- Robert R. Blake and Jane Srygley Mouton, *Building a Dynamic Corporation Through Grid Organization Development* (Reading, Massachusetts: Addison-Wesley Publishing Company, 1969).

Not exactly a replay of the *Managerial Grid* but similar enough not to be on the *must* reading list if one has read the earlier book. Blake and Mouton develop a theme stressing organization rather than individual change, and this makes good sense as well as interesting reading. As in some of their other books this one seems to have a "sales pitch" quality. Reference is made to the book in this monograph simply because it is one of the six books in the Addison-Wesley Series on organization development. Anyone with an active interest in the subject would probably do better by reading *Managerial Grid*.

Table of Contents

This book has a suggested reading list and a subject index.

• Leland P. Bradford, Jack R. Gibb, Kenneth D. Benne, eds., *T-Group Theory and Laboratory Method* (New York: John Wiley and Sons, Inc., 1964).

This is a carefully drawn book which provides solid information pertinent to the leadership and change process. Bradford was for many years the executive director of National Training Laboratories and was in an unusual position to watch the T-group movement develop. His coeditors are respected practitioners and academicians who by knowledge and experience are in a position to discriminate between the significant and the less significant in the field.

The volume reflects the experience and competence of the editors. Articles in the first section of the book are intended to describe and to explain the setting in which the T-group developed, provide some history and delineate some philosophical perspectives from which the T-group as an educational medium can be understood. The second section consists of articles by nine experienced T-group trainers who seek to conceptualize learning goals and processes. The third section compares and contrasts the T-group with other educational media.

The variety and bulk of information provided by respected "toilers in the field" is only meagerly indicated by the table of contents:

Table of Contents

7. Membership and the Learning Process—Leland P. Bradford
8. From Polarization to Paradox—Kenneth D. Benne
9. Patterns and Vicissitudes in T-group Development—Warren G. Bennis
10. Climate for Trust Formation—Jack R. Gibb
11. Psychodynamic Principles Underlying T-group Processes—
    Roy M. Whitman
12. Studying Group Action—Robert R. Blake
13. Training in Conflict Resolution—Murray Horwitz
14. Explorations in Observant Participation—Herbert A. Shephard
15. A Survey of Research on T-groups—Dorthy Stock
16. Training and Therapy—Jerome D. Frank
17. The T-group and the Classroom—Matthew D. Miles
18. A Look to the Future—Leland P. Bradford, Jack R. Gibb,
    Kenneth D. Benne

This book has a subject index.

● Paul Buchanan, ed., *An Approach to Executive Development in Government: The Federal Executive Institute Experience* (Washington, D.C.: National Academy of Public Administration, 1973).

In this unusual publication there is an opportunity to read the thoughts of highly skilled trainers engaged in serious introspection concerning their roles and the prestigious Federal Executive Institute (F.E.I.) during the time it was under the direction of Frank P. Sherwood. The occasion for developing these papers was a colloquium attended by persons who had served on the F.E.I. faculty during the first five years of its existence. The document has special significance to trainers and administrators, for the essays are written by persons who in general have as personal goals the influencing of executives to be able to meet the challenges of massive change.

Table of Contents

Issues and Essays—Paul C. Buchanan
The Federal Executive Institute (from F.E.I.'s 73)
Programs of Institution Building in the Bureaucratic System: One Experience—Frank P. Sherwood
Executive Training and Administrative Theory: Universalistic, Predilection and Diffusionistic—Chester A. Newland
Relevance of Executive Training at the Federal Executive Institute—
Jerome R. Saroff
The Politician and the Bureaucrat: The Problem of Mutual Trust—
T. W. Adams
Can Training Really Carry Over to Work?—William B. Eddy
Laboratory Models and Executive Education at the Federal Executive Education Institute—Richard C. Collins
Education Assumptions in the Federal Executive Institute—Ronald J. Stupak
Profile of the Federal Executive Institute Graduate, Director of Program and Resource Development, Bureau of Executive Manpower
The 1970 Field Trip to Canada: A Follow-Up Report—George A. Warp
My F.E.I. Experience: Some Personal Learnings—Wayne Untereiner

The Prospect of Organizational Development Through Multi-Team Building
—E. J. Jones, Jr.
The Fate of Three Experiments—James R. Roberts
How I Learned to Spell Androgogy!—Logan V. Cockrum
Words at a Gathering: Summary of a Colloquium—Paul C. Buchanan

• Dorwin Cartwright and Alvin Zander, *Group Dynamics: Research and Theory* (Evanston, Illinois: Row, Peterson and Company, 1960).

This formidable book remains as a leading publication covering research on forces at work in groups. Research is reported under six different categories that make up the parts of the text: Introduction to Group Dynamics, Group Cohesiveness, Group Pressures and Group Standards, Individual Motives and Group Goals, Leadership and Group Performance and the Structural Properties of Groups. Each piece of research is reported by the researcher(s) and major thoughts and issues in each part of the book are tied together by comments by Cartwright and Zander.

Any student of group work or group leadership should know of the existence of *Group Dynamics* and its availability as a solid reference resource.

Table of Contents

17. Political Standards in Secondary Groups — Converse and Campbell
18. Overcoming Resistance to Change — Coch and French

Part Four: Individual Motives and Group Goals

19. Individual Motives and Group Goals: Introduction — Cartwright and Zander
20. The Recall and Interrupted Group Tasks: An Experimental Study of Individual Motivation in Relation to Group Goals — Horwitz
21. The Effects of Varied Quality of Group Goal and Group Paths Upon the Individual and His Relation to His Group — Raven and Rietsema
22. The Effects of Cooperation and Competition Upon Group Process — Deutsch
23. The Effects of Facilitative Role Interdependence on Group Functioning — Thomas
24. Organizational Goals and Environment: Goal Setting as an Interaction Process — Thompson and McEwen

Part Five: Leadership and Group Performance

25. Leadership and Group Performance: Introduction — Cartwright and Zander
26. The Behavior of Leaders and Other Group Members — Carter, Haythorn, Shriver, Lanzetta
27. Some Factors in the Selection of Leaders by Members of Small Groups — Kirscht, Lodahl, Haire
28. Leader Behavior and Member Reaction in Three "Social Climates" — White and Lippitt
29. Leadership Practices in Relation to Productivity and Morale — Kahn and Katz
30. Leadership and Crisis — Hamblin
31. The Leader's Psychological Distance and Group Effectiveness — Fiedler
32. The Bases of Social Power — French and Raven
33. Phases in Group Problem Solving — Bales and Strodtbeck

Part Six: The Structural Properties of Groups

34. The Structural Properties of Groups: Introduction — Cartwright and Zander
35. Communications, Patterns in Task Oriented Groups — Bavelas
36. Differentiation of Roles in Task-Oriented Groups — Guetzkow
37. Structural Balance: A Generalization of Heider's Theory — Cartwright and Harary
38. A Formal Theory of Social Power — French
39. The Dynamics of Power — Lippitt, Polansky, Edl, Rosen
40. Power Relations in Three-Person Groups — Mills
41. Communication in Experimentally Created Hierarchies — Kelley
42. Some Effects of Power on the Relations Aong Group Members - Horwitz, Zander, Hymovitch

This book has a subject index. Almost every article is well documented.

- Robert L. Craig and Lester R. Bittel, eds., *Training and Development Handbook* (New York: McGraw-Hill Book Company, 1967).

This is a "how to do it" manual on training of all kinds — from job instruction to laboratory training. It also contains some articles on organizing and managing training programs. Of special interest to those interested in group leadership are sections entitled "Conference Methods" by Louis W. Lerda, "Case Methods" by Paul Pigors, "Role Playing" by Malcolm E. Shaw and "Human Relations Laboratory Training" by Leland P. Bradford and Dorothy J. Mial. Related material which might be of some interest is contained in articles written by Clifford J. Craft, "Management Games," "Training Aids" by Louis S. Goodman and "Use of Consultants" by Lester F. Zerfoss.

This book is worthy of a place in any training library because it provides a good point of departure for the investigation of a wide variety of training activities.

Table of Contents

This book has a subject index.

• Morton Deutsch and Robert M. Krauss, *Theories in Social Psychology* (New York: Basic Books, Inc., 1965).

"Theory is the net man weaves to catch the world of observation — to explain, predict and influence it." (Deutsch and Krauss, p. vii.) This book presents major theories in an expository and critical way. Reading it will not make one an expert, but it will provide an orientation to the major theories and a means of understanding the relationship between them. For administrators and trainers interested in human behavior who have not been steeped in social psychological theory this book is most valuable. For those who have such exposure Deutsch and Krauss still provide a means for the student to "put it all together" theoretically. It does not read like Hemingway.

Table of Contents

This book contains a list of references and a subject index.

154

• William B. Eddy, W. Warner Burke, Vladimir A. Dupre, Oron South, eds., *Behavioral Science and the Manager's Role* (Washington, D.C.: N.T.L. Learning Resources Corporation, 1969).

From time to time the National Training Laboratories issues a "source book" for managers and trainers. *Behavioral Science and the Manager's Role* is such a book. If one looks at the following titles it is clear that the book is organized to examine the relation of behavioral science to business, to look at leadership as an interpersonal process, to consider its relationship to the organizational social system, and finally to become aware of behavioral science approaches to changing and developing organizations.

Table of Contents

1. Behavioral Science and Business
   Valued Man and Organizations — Robert Tannenbaum and Sheldon Davis
   Distortions of Behavioral Science — James V. Clark
2. The Manager as a Person
   The Power to See Ourselves — Paul J. Brouwer
   Toward Becoming a Fully Functioning Person — Carl R. Rogers
   Defenses and the Need to Know — Roger Harrison
   Interpersonal Communication — W. Warner Burke
   The Three Types of Executive Personality — Richard W. Wallen
   Clearing the Air in Human Relations — Barry I. Oshry
3. The Person as a Manager
   Conditions for Manager Motivation — M. Scott Myers
   Dynamics of Leadership: A Look at Some Recent Findings of Behavioral Science Research — James V. Spotts
4. The Manager and the Organization
   The Human Side of Enterprise — Douglas McGregor
   Managerial Grid — Robert Blake, Jane S. Mouton, Alvin C. Bidwell
   Organizational Climate and Individual Growth — Gordon L. Lippitt
   Organizational Revitalization — Warren G. Bennis
   Participative Management: Time for a Second Look — R. C. Albrook
   Today's Problems with Tomorrow's Organization — Chris Argyris
5. Action Steps and Interventions
   Emerging Criteria for Organization Development — Gordon L. Lippitt
   Management Issues in Organization Development — William E. Eddy
   T-groups for Organizational Effectiveness — Chris Argyris
   An Organic Problem Solving Method of Organizational Change — Sheldon A. Davis
   Using Employee Questionnaire Results for Improving Organizations — Howard Baumgaretl
   Union Carbide's Patient Schemers — Gilbert Burck

This book contains a selected bibliography.

• F. E. Emery and E. L. Trist, *Toward a Social Ecology* (London, New York: The Plenum Press, 1973).

Both Emery and Trist have by their research contributed much to our understanding of socio-technical systems. In this very important book they have

155

confronted us with major issues which society and its organizations are now facing and must solve if our quality of life is to be preserved or enhanced.

Emery, the author of Part I, suggests that the appropriate type of planning provides the conceptual base for a future where complexity reduction and early detection of events are essential elements. Active rather than passive adaptation to turbulent environments calls for the emergence of ideal-seeking systems.

In Part II Trist engages the transition of society to post-industrialism. It is necessary, Trist says, to realize that the scientist can no longer lay claim to the whole truth. To make progress we have found that there are other forms of understanding than the "scientism" of the physical sciences. The world cannot survive, that is run, on the inanimate Orwellian model; it must have an integrative strategy that recognizes both the animate and the inanimate. Scientists, professionals, administrators and politicians all have a part to play in developing a mutual science policy. (Emery and Trist, pp. 83-90.)

Trist also suggests the need for domain-based inquiry which links groups of scientists to problem-oriented research in major sections of social concern. Domains would include:

1) resources of the biological and physical environment,
2) productive capability of the economy and
3) quality of life within a society including identification and appraisal of trans-national processes and institutions. (Emery and Trist, pp. 94-102).

Even with domain research and planning Trist sees a possible danger of a society that becomes over-determined. To avoid this danger he suggests a collaborative relationship between social and technical innovation which leads to creation of nonalienated work relationships, development of life careers adapted to the changing character of work, institution building in complex and uncertain environments and diffusion of social science knowledge and capabilities. (Emery and Trist, pp. 103-119.) In the post-industrial society it should be possible to move from the welfare state with its aura of charity and philanthropy to a "service state" which is committed to enhancing the well-being of everyone. (Emery and Trist, pp. 121-157.)

Within this context Trist poses the planner's dilemma: "The greater the degree of change, the greater the need for planning, otherwise precedents of the past could guide the future; but the greater the degree of uncertainty, the greater the likelihood that plans right today will be wrong tomorrow." Trist espouses a three-dimensional cultural model which would be congruent with the post-industrial society. In the model he places 1) cultural values, 2) organizational philosophies and 3) ecological strategies. Under cultural values the model indicates a movement from achievement to self-actualization, self-control to self-expression, independence to inter-dependence, endurance of distress to capacity for joy. Organizational philosophies call for a change from mechanistic to organic forms, competitive to collaborative relations, separate to linked objectives, resources regarded as owned individually to resources regarded as owned by society.

The list is a bit longer for the dimension involving ecological strategies. Here the model suggests a trend away from being responsive to crisis toward

156

being anticipative of crisis, from specific measures toward comprehensive measures, from requiring consent toward requiring participation, from damping conflict toward confronting conflict, from short planning horizons toward long-planning horizons, from detailed central control toward generalized central control, from smaller toward larger local government, from standardized toward innovative administration and from separate services toward coordinated services. (Emery and Trist, p. 186.)

It is likely that the three-dimensional model will lead to a world in which some kind of social insurance will apply to maintenance of life opportunity not simply to loss and disaster. Life space for the individual will be expanded by the addition of more goods, personal resources, amenities and opportunities. Adulthood will find a wider variety of activities. A more complex form of family life is emerging. Total personal income will increase. Families will be engaged in maximizing opportunities to engage in new lifestyles. What is now required is for a person simultaneously to generate, maintain and consume his estate. (Emery and Trist, p. 200.)

In general Trist believes that we are presently living with a cultural-science mismatch. Corrective action will come from a type of planning which gives direction of such standards while at the same time remain flexible. Plans will always be incomplete. A new politics will emerge from the planning process and will lead to the development of a social pluralism which will represent complexity reduction rather than regressive simplification. "The surrender of power is a necessary condition for survival" in a turbulent environment. (Emery and Trist, p. 208.)

In writing *Toward a Social Ecology* Emery and Trist have provided one view of emerging social, cultural and organizational problems and possibilities. They conclude their book with a jointly written appendix which explains the socio-technical system as a source concept.

Table of Contents

13. The Cultural Absence of the Post-Industrial Society
14. Task and Contextual Environments for New Personal Values
15. The Risk-Security Balance and the Burden of Choice
16. Some Planning Toward the Surrender of Power
Appendix: "The Socio-Technical System as a Source Concept," by F. E. Emery and E. L. Trist.
This book contains a list of references and a subject index.

● Thomas Fletcher, ed., *Symposium on Continuing Education for Public Administration (Public Administration Review*, November/December 1973).

Eight authors team up under Fletcher's editorship to discuss new directions in continuing education. Since most of the contributors are interested in how training and development contribute to change the entire symposium should have considerable utility for those working within a participative framework.

Symposium Topics

Introductory Comments — Thomas W. Fletcher
"Give a Damn About Continuing Adult Education in Public Administration"
— Frederick E. Fisher
"Learning from Administrative Experience"— Michael McGill
"Continuing Education for City Managers" — William B. Donaldson
"Training and Education: Trends, Differences and Issues" —
Richard C. Collins
"Education is Not a Place: Connecting Learning and Living" —
Malcolm E. Shaw
"The Realities of Education as a Prescription for Organizational Change"—
Roy G. Gregg and John Van Maanen

● Wendell L. French and Cecil H. Bell, Jr., *Organization Development* (Englewood Cliffs, New Jersey: Prentice Hall, Inc., 1973).

Organization Development is examined from three major perspectives: 1) an introduction to OD including mini-cases of OD usage, a definition of OD and a historical view of how it came into being; 2) the theory and practice of organization development which addresses values and assumptions, types of interventions (team, intergroup, personal and interpersonal and organizational) and the relation of OD, systems concepts and action research; and 3) key considerations and issues. These include (a) systems ramifications such as feedback, job design, career development and training, appraisal and organizational justice; (b) consultant-client relationships; (c) mechanistic and organic systems; and (d) some speculative remarks about the future of OD.

As of this writing this book provides the best available thrust for a systematic understanding of the organization development process. Any person wishing to become acquainted with the nature of OD would do well by starting with this book.

Table of Contents

This book has a subject index.

• Robert T. Golembiewski and Arthur Blumberg, eds., *Sensitivity Training and the Laboratory Approach* (Itasca, Illinois: F. E. Peacock, Publishers, 1970).

It is Golembiewski's declared intention to present a book of readings which attempts to describe and analyze:

1) the laboratory approach and sensitivity training as a learning strategy;
2) various learning strategies that are embodied;
3) concepts that relate to processes and outcomes and
4) ways in which the laboratory approach and sensitivity training can be applied.

There are 37 different articles by an impressive array of authors with the continuity and connection between the writings provided by the editors.

One difficulty of almost any collection of articles is the burden placed on the reader to "put it all together." Golembiewski has attempted to provide a "glue," but in the end there are too many ideas set forth by too many people to make this book into a cohesive whole. Another editor might have chosen other materials, but that would pose the same problem. The value of a book of this kind is to assemble useful information that would otherwise require much research and expenditure of time to find. This is a handy book for the group leader to have at hand, for many of the dilemmas the leader will face are treated somewhere among its pages.

Table of Contents

25. How to Choose Between Strategies of Conflict and Collaboration — Richard E. Walton
26. What is O.D.? — N.T.L. Institute for Applied Behavioral Science
27. Enriching Marriages Through Laboratory Approach: Tentative Steps Toward the 'Open Couple' — Robert T. Golembiewski
28. Magic Circles in the Classroom: Developing Mastery and Healthy Self-Concepts to Support Cognitive and Motor Learning — Harold Bessell
29. Data Feedback and Organizational Change in a School System — Matthew Miles, et al
30. Planned Organizational Change: A Major Emphasis in a Behavioral Approach to Administration — Robert T. Golembiewski
31. Breakthrough in Organization Development — Robert Blake, Jane S. Mouton, L. B. Barnes, Larry E. Greiner
32. Report on First Leadership Teamwork Development Laboratory for Washington, D.C. — H. Curtis Mial
33. Generalizations and Speculations from Experience Related to Laboratory Training Design — Bob Luke and Charles Seashore
34. T-Group Education and Leadership Effectiveness: A Review of the Empiric Literature and a Critical Evaluation — Robert J. House
35. Problems in the Design and Interpretation of Research on Human Relations Training — Roger Harrison
36. Impact of Organizational Training Laboratories Upon the Effectiveness and Interaction of Ongoing Work Groups — Frank Friedlander
37. Some Effects on Business Gaming of Previous Quasi-T-Group Affiliations — Samuel D. Deep, Bernard M. Bass, James A. Vaughn

This book has an author and subject index.

• David Hampton, Charles E. Summer, Ross A. Webber, *Organizational Behavior and the Practice of Management* (Glenview, Illinois: Scott, Foresman and Company, 1968).

There are some obvious "landmark" articles which keep appearing in the better readers. This book has its share of these, but it also has some essays that other collections cited in this monograph do not have. For example, the authors have included "A Theory of Human Motivation" by A. H. Maslow. This is Maslow's early articulation of the hierarchy of need theory. In this book we also find Homan's "Social Behavior and Exchange," McClelland's "The Achievement Motive," Barnard's "The Theory of Authority" and Katz's "Explaining Informal Work Groups in Complex Organizations: The Case for Autonomy in Structure."

One excellent feature of this reader is its evenness of quality. Almost every article has something important to contribute to our thinking on organizational behavior.

Concerning Civil Government — Locke
Law in a Changing Society — Friedman
The Theory of Authority — Barnard
Authority: Its Nature and Motives — Simon, Smithburg, Thompson
The Source of Managerial Authority — O'Donnell
Toward a Theory of Organizational Behavior — Presthus
Types of Power and Status — Goldhammer and Shils
Some Functions of Bureaucratic Rules — Gouldner

Part Three: Managing and Changing Organizations
  Chapter 8. Managing and Changing Organizations by Direct Influence
    Readings:
    How to Choose a Leadership Pattern — Tannenbaum and Schmidt
    Management by Integration and Self-Control — McGregor
    The Headquarters Staff Man in the Role of a Consultant — Kolb
    Management Development as a Process of Influence — Schein
    Sensitivity Training for the Management Team — Tannenbaum, Weschler, Massarik
    Organizational Change — Katz and Kahn

  Chapter 9. Influencing Behavior Through Political Action
    Readings:
    Delegation — Newman, Summer, Warren
    Authority, Discipline and Unity of Command — Fayol
    Decentralization: A Managerial Philosophy — Cordiner
    Functional Authority — Koontz and O'Donnell
    Standing Plans and Their Advantages — Newman
    The Appeals Procedures — Brown
    Strategic Considerations in Planning — Newman

  Chapter 10. Managing and Changing Organizations by Modifying Structure
    Readings:
    Work Flow as the Basis of Organizational Design — Chapple and Sayles
    Reorganizing in an Advertising Agency: A Case Study of a Decrease in Integration — Kover
    The Change Process in Organization: An Applied Anthropology Approach — Sayles
    The Changing of Organizational Behavior Patterns: A Case Study in Decentralization — Lawrence
    Comprehending the Process of Organizational Improvement — Richardson and Zimmerman
This book has a subject index.

• Thomas A. Harris, *I'm O.K., You're O.K.* (New York: Harper and Row, 1967).

"A Practical Guide to Transactional Analysis" (T.A.) is the subtitle of *I'm O.K., You're O.K.*, which fairly well describes the intention of the author. Harris explains sequentially the theoretical genesis, the nature of parent, adult and child behavior and what he terms the four life positions:

I'm not O.K. — you're O.K.
I' m not O.K. — you're not O.K.
I'm O.K. — you're not O.K.
I'm O.K. — you're O.K.

  The remainder of the book addresses how TA concepts can be used by and should be especially useful to the leader and manager who wish to become familiar with T.A. methodology.

Table of Contents

1. Freud, Penfield and Berne
2. Parent, Adult and Child
3. The Four Life Positions
4. We Can Change
5. Analyzing the Transaction
6. How We Differ
7. How We Use Time
8. P-A-C and Marriage
9. P-A-C and Children
10. P-A-C and Adolescence
11. When Is Treatment Necessary?
12. P-A-C and Moral Values
13. Social Implications of P-A-C

There are other books which explain TA concepts and go some depth into TA therapy, but the Harris book gives the subject excellent coverage. If you are one of the many persons who find TA helpful then you should agree that author Thomas A. Harris, is O.K., too.

This book has a subject index.

• John S. Jun and William B. Storm, eds., *Tomorrow's Organizations* (Glenview, Illinois: Scott, Foresman and Company, 1973).

This book addresses the troublesome problem of "where do we go from here?" It includes several articles which are basic to an understanding of change and the process of organizational democracy. For example, the essay by Robert Chin and Kenneth D. Benne, "General Strategies for Effecting Changes in Human Systems," is a management classic. "The Promise of Self-Management" by Elisabeth Mann Borgese is a short but important article which squarely confronts the issue of employee participation. Jun and Storm also include Emery and Trist's base concepts set forth in "The Causal Texture and Organizational Environments." A unique feature of the book emerges in Part III, "New Perspectives in Organizational Theory." Theoretical writings covering 1) open systems, cybernetics and decisions, 2) exchange, motivation and role theory and 3) phenomenology suggest by the very coverage the travail and ferment that is occurring as concerned theoreticians try to grasp the uncertain future.

Table of Contents

Part One: The Different Future
  Chapter 1. Challenges of the Future

The authors conclude with a rather good bibliography pertaining to each major part of the book. In the front a table lists the chapters of this book correlated with contemporary textbooks in organization theory and behavior as well as a table which cross references this particular text with other major textbooks in theory and behavior.

There is a subject index.

• Paul R. Lawrence and Jay W. Lorsch, *Developing Organizations: Diagnosis and Action* (Reading, Massachusetts: Addison-Wesley Publishing Company, 1969).

Lawrence and Lorsch veer away from the usual O.D. model, becoming much more diagnostic in their consulting intervention than might generally be the case. Their research has led them to the development of a "differentiation and integration." The book tells how they go about analyzing the organization — environment — individual interface.

Lawrence and Lorsch have done some very significant research on the problems which evolve between an organization and its environment. This book reflects some of their findings.

Table of Contents

1. Introduction — Defining Organizations and Organizational Development Interface
2. Concepts for Developing Organizations
Systems Analysis
The Differentiation and the Integration Model
Summary of the Conceptual Framework
Determining the Direction for Organizational Development

● Daniel Katz and Robert L. Kahn, *The Social Psychology of Organizations* (New York: John Wiley and Sons, 1966).

One graduate student at the University of Southern California complained that he had been assigned Katz and Kahn in three different courses (behavior, organization theory and systems). He admitted that the book had direct application to all three fields but that he had some difficulty in understanding what was written. Finally he confessed that only after the third reading did the contents of the book emerge with clarity and importance.

Yes, this book is difficult for the unpracticed, but not because of unclear, uninteresting or obtuse writing. Rather it is because of the richness and profuseness of ideas and information that emerge from every page. *The Social Psychology of Organizations* is solid intellectual "food" and almost no "garbage." For those interested in developing a useful and complete sense of the field of organizational psychology this is probably the best book. It is perhaps better to read this book three times than to wander through twenty less sharply focused works one time each.

Open systems theory provides the vehicle for looking at issues which were first raised in Rensis Likert's *New Patterns of Management* and in the theoretical approaches to problems of social structure articulated by Floyd Alpert. Katz and Kahn note the following characteristics which seem to define open systems:

1. importation of energy,
2. throughput which transforms energy,

167

3. output of some product into the environment,
4. systems as cycles of events,
5. negative entropy to arrest the entropic process which moves toward disorganization or death.
6. information, input, negative feedback and the coding process,
7. the steady state of dynamic homeostasis and
8. differentiation.

All in all *The Social Psychology of Organization* is a formidable book which will help an administrator or group leader understand some of the dynamic variables of organization.

Table of Contents

This book has an excellent bibliography and a very complete subject index.

• Kurt Lewin, *Field Theory in Social Science* (New York: Harper and Brothers, 1951).

For those not satisfied with warmed-over knowledge a trip into Kurt Lewin might prove stimulating. Lewin was the major force in the group dynamics movement as well as the conceptualizer of the action research idea. He was called the practical theorist. He believed that action should be the outcome of research, and he demonstrated the importance of participation and involvement in the change process. We have selected this book as a tool book because it contains some of Lewin's thinking on his field theory and gives a comprehensive explanation of the force-field analysis (Chapters IX-X). This book also contains a short but valuable look at the concept of time perspective.

Other books of Lewin are *Resolving Social Conflict*, Harper and Brothers, 1951; *Principles of Topological Psychology*, McGraw-Hill Book Company, 1936; and *Dynamic Theory of Personality*, McGraw-Hill Book Company, 1935.

Lewin's writings have been largely essays growing out of individual investigations and for the most part are collected, translated and edited by others. The Lewin legacy goes far beyond his writings, being manifest largely in the other "giants" he influenced in the growing field of social psychology.

Essays in *Field Theory in Social Science* were written mostly during the last ten years of Lewin's life. They were assembled and edited by Dorwin Cartwright and published posthumously. This book appears to represent the broad range of Lewin's theoretical world even though other of his writings deal with a wide variety of subjects and issues.

Table of Contents

Appendix: Analysis of the Concepts Whole, Differentiation and Unity. This book has a subject index.

● Rensis Likert, *New Patterns of Management* (New York: The McGraw-Hill Book Company, 1961.)

Likert wrote *New Patterns of Management* for an "audience" concerned with problems of organizing human resources and activity. He recognizes that structure and form influence and often dictate human behavior. The research on which Likert's theories are based was generated by the Institute for Social Research at the University of Michigan. While the focus of the volume is largely on business enterprises, public administrators should have little difficulty in examining the general principles of the theory in the light of their own public organizations.

There have been important advances in organizational theory since Likert wrote this book, but he provided a basis for some of the later works and his research findings are perhaps much more important than some of his suggested solutions. The "linking" pin organizational model is certainly an improvement on the traditional bureaucratic organization, but it probably endorses a hierarchical mode that is dysfunctional in a changing organization. The major point for the group leader, whether administrator or trainer, is that almost everything he or she does is influenced and conditioned by the *form* of organization in which the action takes place. This means that the form of organization is of constant concern and in one way or another will occupy a place on the group or organization's agenda.

Table of Contents

` 5. The Effect of Measurements on Management Practices
6. Some General Tends
7. Effective Supervision: An Adaptive and Relative Process
8. An Integrating Principle and Overview
9. Some Empirical Tests of the Newer Theory
10. Voluntary Organizations
11. The Nature of Highly Effective Groups
12. The Interaction-Influence System
13. Function of Measurements
14. A Comparative View of Organizations
15. Looking to the Future

There is a name and subject index.

• Rensis Likert, *The Human Organization* (New York: McGraw-Hill Book Company, 1967).

This book is intended for those who are interested in using the results of applied research to improve the management of the human resources of their enterprise. (p. vii.) Here Likert furthers his explanation of science-based management which he initially proposed in *New Patterns of Management*. One interesting feature of the book is Likert's invitation to the reader to become involved by providing an exercise to complete in Chapter 2. Likert still emphasizes participation as a management mode but for the good of the company and to the end of high productivity rather than for the sake of humanity.

This book does a good job of "walking" the reader through a research process.

Table of Contents

1. New Foundations for the Art of Management
2. A Look at Management Systems
3. Productivity and Labor Relations Under Different Management Systems
4. The Interdependent, Interacting Character of Effective Organization
5. Time: A Key Variable in Evaluating Management Systems
6. Improving General Management by Better Fiscal Management
7. The Need for a General Systems Approach
8. Measurement
9. Human Asset Accounting
10. Achieving Effective Coordination in a Highly Functionalized Company and Elsewhere
11. The Next Step

Appendix I: Correlation Matrix for Items in Table III-1
Appendix II: Profile of Organizational Characteristics
Appendix III: Table of Organizational Variables

Likert has provided a good bibliography as well as a name and subject index.

• Norman R. F. Maier, *Principles of Human Relations* (New York: John Wiley and Sons, Inc., 1952).

Despite the fact that Maier's book was first published in 1952 it contains information that will have considerable utility for present-day group leaders. *Principles of Human Relations* may seem to express rather widely accepted values, but it was one of the early voices which induced many managers to consider the utility of democratic management. The tone of the book is characterized by the quote preceding Chapter I: "There can be no peace or calm in this world until there is full honor and respect — the one individual for another" — Edward Benes.

Coverage ranges from theories of participation to methods of group leadership.

Maier, who apparently originated the "risk technique," sets forth the way in which this method can be used in the process of introducing change in an organization. The author also has an excellent discussion of role playing. Many persons still use the "new truck problem" as a training exercise without being aware that the role playing case was a Maier creation and is thoroughly explained in this book. Another excellent feature is the last chapter on non-directive counseling skill which, as Maier says, is related to both democratic leadership and all types of face-to-face contacts.

Maier has written books on industrial psychology, performance evaluation and role playing. His other books might also be of use to group leaders.

Table of Contents

There is a bibliography that might be worthy of special scrutiny for, although it has only 60 items, many of these are seminal in nature and touch a literature which is sometimes overlooked today. There is a subject index as well.

● Abraham Maslow, *The Psychology of Science* (Chicago: Henry Regnery Company, 1966).

Maslow said a model of science inherited from the impersonal sciences of things, objects, animals and part-processes is "limited and inadequate when we attempt to know and understand whole and individual persons and cultures." Maslow pointedly notes that he is not only speaking out against scientists who deny human values in science just as he opposed others who become "anti-scientific" and even anti-intellectual. He notes that the alternative to science is sometimes sheer freakishness. Therefore in writing this book Maslow wishes it to be understood that he is attempting to enlarge science, not destroy it. "It is not necessary to choose between experiencing and abstracting." (Maslow, p. xvi.)

As one goes into the wonderful world of group dynamics it is well to take heed of Maslow's cautions on "cultishness, uncritical and selfish exaltation of personal experiencing, overreliance on impulsivity, arbitrary whimsicality and emotionality, unskeptical enthusiasm and finally navel watching and solipsism." (Maslow, p. xii.)

Table of Contents

1. Mechanistic and Human Science
2. Acquiring Knowledge of a Person as a Task for the Scientist
3. The Cognitive Needs Under Conditions of Fear and of Courage
4. Safety Science and Growth Science: Science as a Defense
5. Prediction and Control of Persons?
6. Experiential Knowledge and Spectator Knowledge
7. Abstracting and Theorising
8. Comprehensive Science and Simple Word Science
9. Suchness Meaning and Abstractness Meaning
10. Taoistic Science and Controlling Science
11. Interpersonal (I-Thou) Knowledge as a Paradigm for Science
12. Value-Free Science
13. Stages, Levels and Degrees of Knowledge

As one goes into the wonderful world of group dynamics it is well to take heed of Maslow's cautions on "cultishness, uncritical and selfish exaltation of personal experiencing, overreliance on impulsivity, arbitrary whimsicality and emotionality, unskeptical enthusiasm and finally navel watching and solipism." (Maslow, p. xii.)

Table of Contents

1. Mechanistic and Human Science
2. Acquiring Knowledge of a Person as a Task for the Scientist
3. The Cognitive Needs Under Conditions of Fear and of Courage
4. Sfety Science and Growth Science: Science as a Defense
5. Prediction and Control of Persons?
6. Experimental Knowledge and Spectator Knowledge
Abstracting and Theorising
8. Comprehensive Science and Simple Word Science
9. Suchness Meaning and Abstractness Meaning
10. Taoistic Science and Controlling Science

172

11. Interpersonal (I-Thou) Knowledge as a Paradigm for Science
12. Value-Free Science
13. Stages, Levels and Degrees of Knowledge
14. Desacralization and the Resacralization of
This short, easily read book of 151 pages contains a bibliography and an index.

• Michael E. McGill and Melvin E. Horton, Jr., *Action Research Designs for Training and Development* (Washington, D.C.: National Training and Development Press, 1973).

For several years following the death of Kurt Lewin Action Training and Research continued to appear in a wide variety of settings as a major strategy for change. Understandably perhaps the skilled practitioners in the field received their gratifications from effecting social change rather than from writing about it. Though the principle in Action Training and Research might be excused for their "failure to report" it is still unfortunate that the literature has failed to keep up with the practice. Except for a rather good chapter in French and Bell's book on organization development McGill and Horton's *Action Research Designs for Training and Development* marks the first updating of the literature in many years. In this publication the authors present an action research model, give some suggestions for its implementation and provide five case studies for action research projects.

Table of Contents

● Matthew B. Miles, *Learning to Work in Groups* (New York: Teachers College Press, Columbia University, 1967).

Miles manages to take the reader into the intricacies of group work in a most pragmatic manner. While he does touch on theory most of the emphasis is on a normative view and on guides and standards for leaders. The book covers the topics of effective group behavior, the training process, planning for training, training activities, designing training activities and taking the trainer role.

The chapter on training activities should be particularly useful to the beginner who is trying to sharpen leadership skills. Among other things contained in the chapter is a one-page index of topics related to training activities and problems. The index on these pages refers to other parts of the book in which the problem is discussed. Miles continues this unique and useful cross reference approach as he discusses how to study ongoing group behavior. He also sets forth some group methods which have been found useful as a means of increasing group effectiveness.

On pages 194-198- Miles discusses the use of films and provides a selected list of such films.

Table of Contents

1. The Nature of This Book
2. Effective Group Behavior
3. The Training Process
4. Planning for Training
5. Training Activities
6. Designing Training Activities
7. Taking the Training Role
8. Evaluating Training

In addition Miles includes two very valuable appendices. One covers published accounts of training sessions, the other a selected library of resources. These are in addition to a rather extensive bibliography and a subject index.

● Rodney W. Napier and Matti K. Gershenfeld, *Groups: Theory and Experience* (Boston: Houghton Mifflin Company, 1973).

Perhaps the most significant contribution made by this book is the manner in which the material is pulled together for easy use. *Groups: Theory and Experience* does not claim to be a handbook but in many respects might serve the group leader in this respect. The text is rich with examples; illustrations which are intended to highlight theoretical discussion followed by exercises which the group leader might use to enhance learning. For example, the chapter on membership is followed by six exercises designed to help members experience the conflicts of multiple memberships, understand conflicts of representative memberships, learn about reference groups, develop cooperative rather than competitive relationships and understand how interaction and interdependence can increase the attractiveness of the group.

From the standpoint of providing the group leader with information that will be useful in developing a theoretical base as well as providing optional exercises which may be used as a group's need might indicate the Napier and Gershenfeld book has considerable utility.

Table of Contents

Appendix: A Guide for Facilitators. This is a trainer's "how to do it" which includes discussion of some basic understandings for the leader, time as a variable and some types of group methodology.

There is a subject index.

● Donald Nylen, J. Robert Mitchell, Anthony Stout, *Handbook of Staff Development and Human Relations Training: Materials Developed for Use in Africa* (Washington, D.C.: National Training Laboratories Institute for Applied Behavioral Science, no date).

This book should accompany the group leader to every session. It is filled with training exercises, games and role playing situations — in other words resources which a leader can learn to use in groups as appropriate situations arise. All materials have been tested. The fact that they were utilized in a different culture and worked there may give the U.S. trainer even more confidence in their validity since most of the approaches have been generated in this country. The book also provides a variety of training designs which are adaptable to a variety of group settings.

Table of Contents

The bibliography is short but focuses on the problem of group leadership and is particularly valuable for this reason. There is no subject index.

● Carole Pateman, *Participation and Democratic Theory* (Cambridge: The University Press, 1970).

Ms. Pateman is impressed with the irony of a situation in which participation as a value has become so popular while political theorists and political sociologists give the concept such a minimal role. The author devotes a chapter to a critical review of classical theories of democracy. She moves from an examination of classical theory to a review of a "participatory theory of democracy" against which she measures political and industrial trends. This is a compact but important book for those who wish to explore possible futures for a democratic society.

Table of Contents

1. Recent Theories of Democracy and "Classical Myths"
2. A Participatory Theory of Democracy — Rosseau, John Stuart Mill and G. D. H. Cole
3. The Sense of Political Efficacy and Participation in the Work Place
4. "Participation" and "Democracy" in Industry
5. Workers' Self-Management in Yugoslavia
6. Conclusion

Ms. Pateman has an extremely good bibliography which in itself might justify the book. In addition she provides a subject index.

● John M. Pfiffner and Frank P. Sherwood, *Administrative Organization* (Englewood Cliffs, N.J.: Prentice Hall, Inc., 1960).

Administrative Organization has been the "standard work" on organization for the last decade. While the book now desperately needs revision it still is about the only place where one can obtain a comprehensive view of organizations as they are and theories concerning organization.

Table of Contents

Part One: Organization in the Society
1. The Molding of Organization in the Modern Society
2. Complexity of Organization: The Concept of Overlays
3. Complexity of Organization: Man, Groups, Institutions
4. An Introduction to Formal Organization Theory
5. Authority, Policy and Administration as Organization Factors
6. The Metamorphosis of Organization Theory

Part Two: Organization Structure
7. Specialization and Work Division
8. Levels of Specialization and Coordination
9. Coordination at the Top
10. Staff and Functional Aspects
11. Decentralization Pattern
12. Formalization
13. Organization Planning

Part Three: Modifying Systems
14. Introduction to Part III

This book has a subject index.

● J. William Pfeiffer and John E. Jones, *A Handbook of Structural Experience for Human Relations Training*, three volumes (Iowa City, Iowa: University Associate Press, 1969-1971).

Even experienced group leaders tend to fall into ruts which may bring about a boring existence, or worse, the methods which they use have grown comfortable and perhaps outmoded. Pfeiffer and Jones have done a great service in putting together three volumes of activities which may be carried on in groups along with detailed instructions as to how to use them. The author suggests that the leader using these activities is responsible for seeing that the significance of the group experience lies in the applicability of the learning which may be derived from them.

With this caveat the authors provide 74 different ways (in all three volumes) to introduce meaningful learning experiences in groups. The address of University Associates Press is P.O. Box 615, Iowa City, Iowa. This series is virtually a must for group leaders.

Volume I:
Preface
Introduction
1. Listening and Inferring: A Getting-Acquainted Activity
2. Two-Four-Eight: Building Teams
3. T-P Leadership Questionnaire: An Assessment of Style
4. One-Way, Two-Way: A Communications Experiment
5. Who Am I?: A Getting-Acquainted Activity
6. Group-On-Group: A Feedback Experience
7. Broken Squares: Nonverbal Problem-Solving
8. Listening Triads: Building Communications Skills
9. Committee Meeting: Demonstrating Hidden Agendas
10. Process Observation: A Guide
11. Top Problems: A Consensus-Seeking Task
12. Choosing A Color: A Multiple-Role-Play
13. Johari Window: An Experience in Self-Disclosure and Feedback
14. Conflict Resolution: A Collection of Tasks
15. Residence Halls: A Consensus-Seeking Task
16. Fantasies: Suggestions for Individuals and Groups
17. Leveling: Giving and Receiving Adverse Feedback
18. Dependency-Intimacy: A Feedback Experience
19. Awareness Expansion: A Potpourri
20. Graphics: Self-Disclosure Activities

At the end of Volume II there is a bibliography of additional resources.
Volume III also carries a bibliography of additional resources.
- Earl G. Planty and J. Thomas Freeston, *Developing Management Ability* (New York: The Ronald Press Company, 1954).

Developing Management Ability was a training best-seller in its day and is still a very useful book for managers, group leaders or trainers. The book bulges with specifics. It deals with nature, methods and type of development. Although the book is divided into three parts and 18 chapters the text is developed around 600 questions and answers according to the dust jacket. These questions are those actually asked of the authors by businessmen interested in the subject of development.

Planty and Freeston did not write this book as a text but as a working tool for managers and trainers. In the preface they noted that they respected differences in points of view but were not themselves timid or uncertain about their position on methods. This brash forthrightness is one of the factors that contributes to manager understanding and helps show how the training strategy becomes an integral part of day-to-day operation. The "methods" discussion is very helpful to the group leader.

Table of Contents

Part Five: Evaluation
   31. Evaluating Development Activities
Planty and Freeston have a 104-item bibliography and a subject index.

● Carl R. Rogers and William R. Coulson, eds., *Freedom to Learn* (Columbus, Ohio: Charles E. Merrill Publishing Company, 1969).

In *Freedom to Learn* Carl R. Rogers makes his statement on the educational process. "Education today is faced with incredible challenges, different from, and more serious than, it has ever met in its long history." Rogers is concerned about our ability to prepare people to live with change, racial tensions, international problems, atomic destruction and unrest. (p. vi) Rogers admits to a sense of urgency he felt in preparing the manuscript which was derived from his desire to contribute whatever he could to teachers and educators in what he sees as a time of fearful crisis.

The first part of the book is intended to be highly practical in that it points the way to experimentation in learning. Although Rogers aims this at the classroom what he is saying has direct application to the functioning of work groups.

Finally the focus changes to the personal and philosophical ramifications of the educational approach, and the book concludes with a suggested program for bringing about self-directed change.

Table of Contents

   This book carries an annotated bibliography and a subject index.

● Carl R. Rogers, *Client Centered Therapy* (New York: Houghton-Mifflin Company, paperback, 1965).

Client Centered Therapy heads the list of readings I consider appropriate, useful and necessary for the group leader. The "propositions" posed in Chapter II, "A Theory of Personality and Behavior," form the essential theoretical foundation for the type of group leadership proposed in this monograph. The other sections of the book are also very important. Part I, in which Rogers considers "A Current View of Client Centered Therapy," talks about the character of the client centeredness, the importance of the counselor's orientation, the client's relationship, the process itself and some questions raised by his viewpoints.

Client Centered Therapy includes chapters on Play Therapy and Group Centered Leadership in Administration. These particular three chapters are authored by Elaine Dorfman, Nicholas Hobbs and Thomas Gordon, respectively. Rogers does two other chapters on Applications: "Student-Centered Teaching" and the "Training of Counselors and Therapists."

Throughout the book the reader is provided with verbatim transcripts of actual counseling situations which illustrate the theoretical points raised by the author. Rogers does indeed present us with a practical theory and an opportunity to consider theoretical practice.

Table of Contents

Part One: A Current View of Client Centered Therapy
 1. The Developing Character of Client Centered Therapy
 2. The Attitude and Orientation of the Counselor
 3. The Therapeutic Relationship as Experienced by the Client
 4. The Process of Therapy
 5. Three Questions Raised by Other Viewpoints: Transference, Diagnosis, Applicability
Part Two: The Application of Client Centered Therapy
 6. Play Theory — Elaine Dorfman
 7. Group Centered Psychotherapy — Nicholas Hobbs
 8. Group Centered Leadership and Administration — Thomas Gordon
 9. Student Centered Teaching
 10. The Training of Counselors and Therapists
Part Three: Implications for Psychological Theory
 11. A Theory of Personality and Behavior
Rogers provides 228 different references and has prepared a subject index.

● Theodore Reik, *Listening With the Third Ear* (New York: The Grove Press, 1948).

This entire book is devoted to listening. It is recommended as must reading for the developing group leader. True, the emphasis is on listening in the psychoanalytic situation, but the process is so clearly explicated that one can see the direct application to almost all interpersonal situations. Reik writes in a delightful manner and although the book exceeds 500 pages reading it is recreational as well as educational.

Those who find 500 pages overwhelming and who are not titillated by Reik's fascinating anecdotes nor his fine turn of phrase at least owe themselves exposure to the chapters entitled "The Third Ear," "Free Floating Attention," and "Who Am I?"

Table of Contents

• Edgar H. Schein, *Organizational Psychology* (Englewood Cliffs, N.J.: Prentice Hall, Inc., 1965).

This book is tightly written and is quickly read. It was Schein's declared intention to provide some thoughts which would contribute to the ultimate shape of the field of organizational psychology. In this attempt he has extracted pertinent and useful materials from the current fields of industrial psychology, industrial sociology and social psychology. Schein does not deal with theory building, nor does he discuss some issues in great depth. He does provide a cognitive map of the field as well as bibliographic direction for those wishing to explore further any of the book's major topical areas.

Table of Contents

This book provides a short, high-quality bibliography and a subject index.

- Edgar H. Schein, *Process Consultation: Its Role in Organization Development* (Reading, Massachusetts: Addison-Wesley Publishing Company, 1969).

In this book in the Addison-Wesley Series Schein develops perspectives on process consultation. Schein brings the reader into the working situation with case illustrations and a discussion of roles which might be appropriate for a consultant. According to Schein process consultation involves the client in a period of joint consultation. "Process consultation is a set of activities on the part of the consultant which help the client to perceive, understand and act upon process events which occur in the client's environment." (Schein, p. 9.) The consultant under such conditions is willing to help the client identify problems and to point up situations which require improvement.

Schein has said that process consultation assumes the following:

1. Managers often need help for diagnosing problems when they do not know what is wrong.

2. Managers have a problem of knowing what kinds of helps consultants can give and what kind of help to seek.

3. Most managers would like to improve things, but they need help in determining what to improve and how to improve it.

4. It is possible for organizations to be more effective if they learn to diagnose their own strengths and weaknesses.

5. A consultant needs to work jointly with members of the organization who know the culture.

6. Although decision must remain in the hands of the client the consultant's role is to help the client learn to see problems for himself and to share in the diagnosis as well as in generating a remedy.

7. The consultant provides new and challenging alternatives for the client's consideration.

8. The process consultant should be expert in how to *diagnose* and how to *establish effective helping relationships* and be able to pass on both of these skills. (Schein, p. 8.)

Table of Contents

This book provides a list of references and also three appendices that are of some importance:
Memo 1: Some Comments on Internal Auditing and the Control Program
Memo 2: Organization
Memo 3: Erosion of Rationality: One Hazard of Internal Competition on Product Planning

Table of Contents

This volume has an extensive bibliography and a subject index.

● Harry Stack Sullivan, *The Psychiatric Interview* (New York: W. W. Norton & Company, Inc., 1954).

The works of Sullivan are "gold mines" for those interested in the processes of human behavior. Sullivan was a psychiatrist, but much of what he has written has interest and application to non-psychiatric situations. Sullivan does an outstanding job in this book of taking the reader through a psychiatric interview, pausing now and then to explain what is happening and what he (Sullivan) is trying to elicit from the interviewee. This is an uncommonly well-conceptualized book and very useful to anyone operating in a "change agent" role.

Table of Contents

4. Early Stages of the Interview
5. The Detailed Inquiry: The Theoretical Setting
6. The Interview Process
7. The Developmental History as a Frame of Reference in the Detailed Inquiry
8. Diagnostic Signs and Patterns of Mental Disorder, Mild and Severe
9. The Termination of the Interview
10. Problems of Communication in the Interview

Since this book is a posthumous one compiled from Sullivan's lectures there are no listed references. There is a subject index.

• Edgar H. Schein and Warren G. Bennis, *Personal and Organizational Change Through Group Methods* (New York: John Wiley and Sons, Inc., 1965).

According to the authors this "book is written for all those individuals who are interested in the complicated social and psychological processes of change and for all those individuals interested in controlling the outcomes of these change processes." (Schein and Bennis, p. 3.) Schein and Bennis suggest that laboratory training offers an appropriate means of helping people deal with some of the core crises facing society. Organizations, they say, must develop mechanisms for communications and collaboration as well as better mechanisms for coping with externally induced stress.

In addition to the section designed to answer the question "What is Laboratory Training?" and the final section entitled "A Theory of Learning Through Laboratory Training" the book includes articles by a number of other authors.

Table of Contents

Part One: What is Laboratory Training?
  Chapter 1. Introduction
  Chapter 2. What is Laboratory Training: Description of A Typical Residential Laboratory
  Chapter 3. Overview of Laboratory Training
Part Two: The Use of Laboratory Training
  Chapter 4. Variations of Laboratory Training
  Chapter 5. The Design of One-Week Laboratories — Roger Harrison and Barry Osdry
  Chapter 6. Sensitivity Training and Being Motivated — J. F. T. Bugental and Robert Tannenbaum
  Chapter 7. The Uses of the Laboratory Method in the Psychiatric Hospital
    Section A. The Patient Training Laboratory, An Adaptation of the Instrumented Training Laboratory — Robert Morton
    Section B. Follow-Up Evaluation of Human Relations Training for Psychiatric Patients — D. L. Johnson, P. G. Hanson, T. Rothus, Robert B. Morton, F. A. Lyle, R. Moyer
  Chapter 8. The Nine, Nine Approach for Increasing Organizational Productivity — Robert A. Blake and Jane Srygley Mouton
  Chapter 9. Sensitivity Training and Community Development — Donald C. Klein

In addition to the selected bibliography the authors include a list of references and a subject index.

● Laurence N. Solomon and Betty Berson, eds., *New Perspectives on Encounter Groups* (San Francisco: Jossey-Bass, Inc., Publishers, 1971).

In this volume the focus is exclusively on the group. In the preface the authors indicate that the idea for the book was generated while both were on the staff of the Western Behavioral Science Institute. The interest in encounter, suggest Solomon and Berson, may be a cultural attempt to meet the isolation of contemporary life. Essays in the book cover empirical research and decriptive pieces about approaches taken in a variety of groups. The quality of the articles is quite variable, but each topical area in the book has relevance to the group leader.

● Herbert A. Thelen, *Dynamics of Groups at Work* (Chicago: The University of Chicago Press, 1954).

Although more than 20 years have passed since the writing of this book, its usefulness has not diminished. Thelen has provided the group leader with much information that is still unobtainable elsewhere. What he has written holds up as well now as when it was written. By some definitions the book becomes a classic and at least approaches the venerable status of a "standard work." In fact there is a good deal of comfort to be derived from the thought that later group experience and research have substantiated rather than detracted from the Thelen position.

In the preface Thelen tells us that the face-to-face group work on a problem is the meeting ground of individual and society. In the group personality is socialized, and it is through groups that society is changed and adapted to its times. These two prospects are aspects of the same phenomenon. Thelen assumes that basic principles and understanding of groups can be found in successful practice of teaching, traincng, administration and public meetings so he devotes part of the book to technologies derived from experience in such settings. In Part Two of the book Thelen examines concepts useful in thinking about group activity regardless of social purpose.

Thelen then relates his work theoretically to the work of Lawrence F. Foster, R. W. Tyler, Carl Rogers, Kurt Lewin, John Dewey and R. W. Bion. The book is theoretically sound and of great practical use.

Table of Contents

Part One: Six Technologies
1. Rebuilding the Community Through Citizen Action
2. Educating Children Through Need-Meeting Activity
3. Developing the School Through Faculty Self-Training
4. Administration and Management: Group Responsibility and Individual Autonomy
5. Training for Group Participation: The Laboratory Method
6. Effective Meanings: Principles and Procedures

Part Two: Explanation
7. Membership: The Groups Within
8. Integration: Evaluating and Acting
9. Reality: Factors in the Problem Situation
10. Control: Developing the Group Culture
11. Leadership: Coordinating Effort Toward Group Goals
12. Community: The Context of Group Operation

This book has a section of selected readings and a subject index.

• John Van Maanen, *The Process of Program Evaluation* (Washington, D.C.: National Training and Development Service Press, 1973).

One of the cloying concerns of group leaders is over-evaluation. Evaluation and feedback are an integral part of group life. The need for evaluation of programs becomes increasingly clear as we engage an uncertain future. We worry not only whether we accomplished what we set out to do, but also whether in the process we set in motion unknown forces which stimulated unintended consequences, both desirable and undesirable. For the public administrator the Van Maanan monograph may be the most insightful and practical examination of program evaluation yet written. It recognizes the needs for examining both covert and hidden processes and for relating evaluation to the political process.

Table of Contents

1. Introduction
   Evaluation for Whom?
   Evaluation by Whom?
   Evaluation and Research: Point and Counterpoint
2. An Overview: Evaluation Model
   Evaluation in Everyday Life
   A Process Model of Evaluation
   Prelude
3. The Evaluation Questions
   Starting Out
   Specification of Objectives
   Specification of the Program

This monograph contains two appendices: one a note on confidentiality; the other, a very good selected bibliography including references on evaluation and its techniques, standardized measures, survey research (questionnaire development and design), interviewing and observational techniques.

- Dwight Waldo, ed., *Symposium on Organization Development,* (Public Administration Review, March/April, 1974).

This issue adds both theory and description of Methodology to the Organization Development Literature. Articles contained in it are not yet to be found elsewhere. George Lehner's description of training team-building leaders is particularly relevant to the general subject-matter of this monograph.

Symposium Topics

"History of Organization Development," Michael McGill.
"Action Training and Research: Something Old and Something New,"
   Neely Gardner
"Human Resources Development in O.D.," Malcolm E. Knowles
"Training Trainers in the Process of Team Building," George Lehner
"The Future of Organization Development," Larry Kirkhart and
   Orian White

- Richard E. Walton, *Interpersonal Peacemaking: Confrontation and Third-Party Consultation* (Reading, Massachusetts: Addison-Wesley Publishing Company, Inc., 1969).

Walton's book is one of the more specific in the Addison-Wesley Series. Of third-party consultation Walton says, "It may work to ensure motivation on the part of principals, create parity in their situational power, synchronize their negative and positive moves, provide the social support and process expertise that enhance openness." (Walton, Preface v).

After an introductory chapter Walton introduces three case studies. The first examines the process of negotiating a relationship; the second, confronting a deeply felt conflict; and the third, searching for an accommodation. Thereafter Walton walks through the model and the methodology which apply to the third-party consultation process. This is a very useful tool book for the group leader.

Table of Contents

1. Introduction
2. Bill-Lloyd: Negotiating a Relationship
3. Mac-Sy: Confronting a Deeply Felt Conflict
4. Fred-Charles: Searching for An Accommodation
5. Diagnostic Model of Interpersonal Conflict
6. Confrontations and Strategic Third-Party Functions
7. Third-Party Interventions and Tactical Choices
8. Third-Party Attributes
9. Summary and Conclusions

This book contains no subject index.

Some Interesting Resource Articles

• Elisabeth Mann Borgese, "The Promise of Self-Management," *The Center Magazine*, May/June 1972.

There are universal experiences working in the direction of self-management. These experiences include the increase of diffuse ownership, environmental and resource pressure and the approach of a trans-national era. We will, says this essayist, live in an open order with everybody being part of a number of overlapping sub-systems with individuals organizing work, leisure and economic, cultural and spiritual life and moving freely within these sub-systems.

• Isidor Chein, Stuart W. Cook, John Harding, "The Field of Action Research," *The American Psychologist*, 3:43, 1948.

Here is a conceptual presentation of action research. It is one among very few existing references and is often quoted particularly in terms of four types of action research: diagnostic, participant, empirical and experimental.

• Sheldon Davis, "An Organic Problem Solving Method of Organizational Change," *The Journal of Applied Behavioral Science*, Vol. 3, No. 1, January/February/March, 1967, pp. 3-24.

In this article Davis describes the values and processes of O.D. activities in T.R.W. Systems. T.R.W. places a heavy emphasis on confrontation and training in an effort to improve the organization's cultures. The improvement comes out of the better quality of working relationships between individuals and groups.

- Bertram M. Gross, "Friendly Fascism," *Social Policy*, November/December 1970.

"We must accept the possibility that in this decade in our America — despite all we may love and admire in it — may have a rendezvous with fascism." (Gross, p. 44) It will be a new look fascism operating with cybernetic technology, nationwide urbanism, electronic mass media and welfare state comfort. This state may arrive, not by revolution but gradually through our present institutions. Thus speculates Gross in an extremely serious and thought-provoking essay.

- A. H. Maslow, "A Theory of Human Motivation," *Psychological Review*, Vol. 50, 1943. pp. 370-396.

In this article we find the kernel of Maslow's theories of motivation including a description of the now widely known "hierachy of needs."

- Goodwin, Watson, "Resistance to Change," *Concepts for Social Change*, Vol. 1 (Washington, D.C.: National Training Laboratories, 1966).

An important detailing of the various dimensions of resistance to change which provides an elaboration on Lewin's force-field analysis.

Index

195

The National Training and Development Service (NTDS) for State and Local Government is a nonprofit organization whose purpose is to help increase the problem solving capabilities of state, county and municipal elected and appointed officials. Its training and development programs are designed to strengthen the leadership abilities of individuals and organizations and to help them develop better decision making capabilities.

NTDS began its activities in May 1972 and was created by the major public interest groups serving state and local government. They are:

Council of State Governments
International City Management
   Association
National Association of Counties
National Governors' Conference
National League of Cities
National Legislative Conference
U.S. Conference of Mayors

NTDS is financed by the Intergovernmental Personnel Act and the Ford Foundation. State and local governments participating in NTDS programs also provide financial support.

Participants attend NTDS programs without regard to race, color, national origin, sex, religion, creed or political affiliation.